ULTIMATE RECORD BREAKING DEST

ULTIMATE REG

DESTIN

ORD BREAKING
ATIONS

The World's Largest, Highest and Most Extreme Places

Samantha Wilson

NEW
HOLLAND

CONTENTS

1	Hang Son Doong Cave	26	Westray	51	Lake Titicaca	76	Eastern State Penitentiary
2	Millau Viaduct	27	Lake Baikal	52	Schönbrunn Zoo	77	Dinosaur Provincial Park
3	Salar De Uyuni	28	Hassan II Mosque	53	General Sherman	78	Glenwood Hot Springs
4	309 AMARG	29	Cherrapunji & Mawsynram	54	Kolukkumalai	79	Lord Howe Island Group
5	Sermeq Kujalleq	30	Lalibela	55	Lake Turkana	80	Bodega Colomé
6	Chernobyl and Pripyat	31	Cotahuasi	56	Burj Khalifa	81	Mongolia
7	Mount Thor	32	Ironbridge	57	The Sundarbans	82	Ashmolean Museum
8	USS Oriskany	33	The Empty Quarter	58	Sublimotion	83	Ometepe
9	The Dead Sea	34	San Pedro Sula	59	Atacama Desert	84	Giant Buddha of Leshan
10	Bishop Rock	35	Great Blue Hole	60	Ulm Minster	85	Molokai
11	The Namib Desert	36	Bucharest Palace of Parliament	61	Oymyakon	86	Prague Castle
12	Ilha Grande	37	Crater Lake	62	Tyne Cot Cemetery	87	Xinjiang
13	Tristan Da Cunha	38	Highway 1 Australia	63	Frying Pan Lake	88	Grand Bazaar
14	Smithsonian Institution	39	Moyenne Island	64	Potala Palace	89	Ushuaia
15	Ngorongoro Crater	40	Abu Simbel	65	Cox's Bazar	90	Keukenhof
16	Monaco	41	Mosquito Bay	66	Qinghai-Tibet Railway	91	Bay of Fundy
17	Mount Stromboli	42	Eden Project	67	Ngerulmud	92	Haifa
18	Great Mosque of Djenné	43	Mount Chimborazo	68	King Fahd Fountain	93	Victoria Falls
19	Daintree	44	ICEHOTEL	69	The Congo River	94	Via Appia
20	The American Queen	45	Puerto Princesa	70	Tower of Hercules	95	Yellowstone National Park
21	Dallol	46	Borobudur	71	El Alto / La Paz	96	Lærdal Tunnel
22	San Alfonso del Mar	47	Kvarken Archipelago	72	Avenida 9 de Julio	97	The Pantanal
23	Maldives	48	The Canton Tower	73	East Rennell	98	Grand Canal
24	MUSA Cancun	49	Fraser Island	74	Cedar Avenue of Nikkō	99	The 'Falkirk Triangle'
25	Angel Falls	50	El Sobrino de Botín	75	Longyearbyen	100	KwaZulu Natal Coast

THE QUEST FOR THE BEST

Since tweed-coated, leather-booted intrepid explorers of yesteryear first embarked on journeys into the true unknown, world exploration has driven a passion within us. Charles Darwin's unquenchable curiosity landed him in the Galapagos Islands and rewarded us with the theory of evolution. Fridtjof Nansen, the grandfather of polar exploration was the first to cross the Arctic Ocean, sailing further north than any other man before him. The names Captain Cook, Marco Polo and Christopher Columbus ignite awe and a childlike sense of wonderment within us, their dusty footprints leading us down that path less travelled.

Yet the great explorers have left more of a legacy than the scientific and geographical discoveries they were famed for. They dangled tantalising adventures in front of us and ignited a deep curiosity in the world in which we live, a desire to see further, experience more and achieve the impossible. Modern day explorers now fuel our wanderlust, from Michael Palin's journeys around the world in 80 days to Richard Branson's hot air balloon escapades. We gasp, heart in mouth, as Felix Baumgartner jumps from space and sit riveted as David Attenborough transports us into nature's den.

So why do we leave the comforts of home, the people we know and the culture we understand? Perhaps it's simply to relax, to put some space between us and home, clear the mind of daily stresses and take a break from all that is normal. Perhaps it's to broaden the mind, challenge what we know, open our eyes to other cultures, and in doing so envisage new possibilities and unshackle our thoughts. Or perhaps it's simply that we humans are a migratory species fulfilling an intuitive thrill and subconscious drive that stems from our hunter-gatherer roots. More likely we travel to appreciate the new and the different, to enjoy the variety and beauty of planet earth and to find ourselves, lose ourselves and to challenge ourselves. And we search for a way to make sense of our place in this big old world, to somehow put it all into some perspective.

The world is interminably fascinating – whether you're cruising Greenland's fjords, unwinding in a Beijing spa or going in search of ancient rock art in Botswana. Beauty is subjective and what one adores another will abhor. Anointing a destination 'the best' is a bold step, for what one perceives as perfection might not quite tickle the travel taste buds of another. Yet it is human nature to push the limits, a natural instinct which drives us to succeed and achieve, and our attitude to travel is no different.

'Twenty years from now you will be more disappointed by the things that you didn't do than by the ones you did do. So throw off the bowlines. Sail away from the safe harbor. Catch the trade winds in your sails. Explore. Dream. Discover.'

– Mark Twain

Experiencing the world's largest, oldest, highest or most extreme destinations – those that are truly and factually unsurpassable – provides us with an undeniable sense of achievement. To stand in front of the majestic Prague Castle with its turrets and opulence and know that it is the biggest on planet earth is a special feeling. To walk along the shores of the Dead Sea and know there is no lower place in the world, or to swim alongside a gentle whale shark and look into the eyes of the ocean's largest fish goes some way to putting it all in perspective. Only then, at the pinnacle of what the world has to offer, can you begin to fathom the sheer vastness and variety of it all.

HANG SON DOONG CAVE
VIETNAM

Deep in the remote Vietnamese jungle, buried for centuries below a tangle of inhospitable vegetation and known only to the resident monkeys and flying foxes, lays a gargantuan grotto to beat all others – the world's largest cave.

In 1991, a lone farmer stumbled across a gaping hole in the cave-pocketed limestone mountains near the border with Laos. Peering into the dark abyss, he was met with the deafening roar of an underground river raging below, echoing off the vast chamber walls. Not until 2009, however, did the first team of explorers venture deep underground to find one of the planet's best-kept and most astounding secrets.

Imagine a cave large enough to fit a city street in – complete with 40-storey skyscrapers – and you're imaging just one of Hang Son Doong's vast chambers. Measuring up to 180 metres (590 feet) in height, 200 metres (656 feet) in width and 5.6 miles (9 kilometres) in length it is an otherworldly place where 80 metre (262 feet) high stalagmites tower into the dark, a fierce river gushes through and waterfalls pour down the walls.

For Hang Son Doong isn't just a gaping hole in the earth's crust, but a living ecosystem untouched for millions of years, a micro-world of bizarre formations and unique ecological features. Two vast skylights allow light to flood the cave floor giving life to a jungle with trees 30 metres (98 feet) tall and previously undiscovered plant and animal species. Fields of algae from ancient pools blanket parts of the cave walls, 300 million year-old fossils rest untouched, and thousands of baseball-sized calcium cave 'pearls' rest on the cave floor.

The cave's discovery is new and raw, its secrets still being discovered. The Vietnamese government has granted a limited number of visitor permits, allowing would-be explorers the chance to be one of the first to delve into Hang Son Doong's depths on an organised excursion. While you don't need to be an intrepid explorer, it isn't for the faint-hearted. A visit begins with a six hour jungle trek and an 80 metre (262 feet) rappel into the mouth of the cave. Yet a trip into what must surely be one of the planet's last great natural discoveries is to experience a prehistoric world untouched by man – a true-life Indiana Jones adventure of gargantuan proportions.

Did You Know?

Until the discovery of Hang Son Doong, the previous record-holder was Deer Cave in Malaysian Borneo. At an average 91 by 91 metres (298 by 298 feet) in size it still tops Hang Son Doong's 80 by 80 metre (262 by 262 feet) average, but its 1.2 miles (2 kilometres) of length is dwarfed by its Vietnamese competitor, which is five times larger. While Hang Son Doong might be the largest, it is by no means the longest with the record going to Mammoth Cave in Kentucky, USA which disappears 403 miles (650 kilometres) into the earth.

Take Me There

How to Visit: Six-day trekking tours which include three nights camping inside the cave can be arranged through Oxalis Adventures. Many of the guides were on the very first exploration trip into the cave. Groups are a maximum of six and there are limited permits per year (tours began in 2014).

Further Information: Tours can be arranged through Oxalis Adventures **www.oxalis.com.vn** and for further information on Hang Son Doong visit **www.sondoongcave.org**.

THE MILLAU VIADUCT
FRANCE

In the Tarn Valley a sense of serenity and timelessness fills the air. The great river bubbles through the lush landscape, snaking its way gently past picturesque medieval towns with their Gothic churches and grand hilltop châteaux. Yet the laid-back idyll of this quaint and historic region of France's Languedoc was once shattered by the thunder of traffic that coursed through the gorge en route from Paris to Spain's Mediterranean coast. That was, however, until 2004 when the Millau Viaduct was inaugurated and the world's tallest bridge restored peace once again to the Tarn Valley.

The bridge is a jaw-dropping feat of engineering. The €400 million behemoth is part of La Méridienne, the A75 motorway which links Clermont-Ferrand with Béziers and Narbonne, and towers above the canyon below it. Like a great, delicate sail it stands on just seven pillars – higher even than the Eiffel Tower – and stretches 2,460 metres (8.070 feet) across the green valley carved from the limestone plateau. The bridge's road platform, which affords motorists a spectacular yet stomach-lurching view 270 metres (890 feet) down to the ground below, ranks it the 12th highest bridge deck in the world.

Despite the antiquity of the region, where tales of the Knights Templar come to life and turreted fortresses cling to rocky spurs, the viaduct has become a living and harmonious part of the landscape. Kayaks and canoes drift beneath and hikers watch vultures and falcons soar within its arms as they explore the wild scenery of the Parc Naturel Régional des Grands Causses. It forms a contrasting background to the traditional towns of the Tarn Valley, from the beautiful Brousse-le-Château with its Middle Age pebbled streets to Roquefort, home of the famous blue cheese, and Millau, the gateway to the region famed for its art and history (it even offers open-top bus tours to the bridge these days).

While the bridge is never far from sight, getting up close to this feat of modern architecture allows for some impressive panoramic views. The open-air Viaduc Espace Info exhibition allows visitors to climb inside the P2 pillar, the tallest in the world; the Viaduc Expo rest area offers an incredible panorama; while down river from Millau the town of Peyre, with its troglodyte houses and Romanesque church, proffers amazing vistas. So delve into the nature, history and tradition of the Averyon Region and take a boat trip, hike, quad bike, canoe or even hang-glide above what is often hailed one of the world's greatest engineering achievements.

Did You Know?

Owing its origins to the town of the same name, Roquefort is one of the oldest cheeses in the world. It is believed to have been first eaten in about 79AD and under EU law only cheeses aged in the Combalou caves can call themselves Roquefort.

Take Me There

How to Visit: The Millau Viaduct and Tarn Valley are within the Averyon region of Languedoc which can be accessed from the Paris to Spain motorway or from the nearby international airport of Montpellier.

Further Information: The official website of the Millau Viaduct **www.leviaducdemillau.com** offers plenty of information on the bridge itself as well as the Viaduc Espace Info and Viaduc Expo, while the Aveyron Tourism **www.tourisme-aveyron.com** provides travel information to the region.

SALAR DE UYUNI
BOLIVIA

At 3,656 metres (11,995 feet) above sea level in Bolivia's mountain plateau there is a vast mirror, a place where the sky and the land meet in a line that is blurred beyond the capabilities of the human eye. Puffy white clouds are everywhere, reflected underfoot in the thin film of water that often covers the landscape and seemingly just out of arms reach in the cold blue skies above. It is an otherworldly place, often dubbed 'Heaven on Earth', and the world's flattest place, a mesmerising optical illusion created by a vast and ancient salt pan that sits in the foothills of the Andes. At 4,086 square miles (10,582 square kilometres), the Salar De Uyuni is not only the flattest place in the world but also the largest salt flat on earth.

In the dry season the salt flats stretch for mile after mile in a 360 degree panorama, a deep, rock-hard lake of blinding white patterned with a mesh of small raised pentagons reminiscent of a giant salty beehive. It is devoid of any vegetation except for the odd sturdy cactus that grows on the rocky outcrop of Isla del Pescado, a fish-shaped island that rises out of the sea of salt.

Travellers seem to float effortlessly through the strange wonderland, a land so flat that NASA uses it to calibrate satellite orbits. The Salar de Uyuni was once part of a prehistoric lake that covered most of Bolivia, which when it dried up left behind several salt pans and multi-coloured lagoons, which today are frequented by migrating flamingos. Despite its tourist appeal, where 4x4 tours of the flats and Bolivia's Atacama Desert trundle out of the town of Uyuni, the Salar is also a crucial source of lithium. The fairly recent discovery that up to 70% of the world's lithium reserves are here has seen a rise in its extraction.

Uyuni is the gateway to the salt flats, a rough-around-the-edges mining town that was once a transport hub for minerals extracted from the Andes. Salt-battered buses hurtle around town, there is a busy street market frequented by traditionally-clad locals, and llama caravans often arrive from neighbouring villages. On the outskirts of town, in an arid and unmarked graveyard, trains sit abandoned in their dozens, relics of a bygone mining era, and a fascinating place to clamber atop 19th century locomotives.

Did You Know?

Tours to the Salar de Uyuni are not for the faint-hearted and the climate and conditions can be harsh. For those in search of a bit of pampering however, the Palacio de Sal (Salt Palace) Hotel offers a luxury stay in a building made completely of salt, from the floors to the beds. It is the world's first – and currently only – salt hotel.

Take Me There

How to Visit: Buses from La Paz, Potosí and other Bolivian towns arrive in Uyuni for the start of 4x4 jeep tours. Tours range from one to five days ending up back in Uyuni or in Tupiza.

Further Information: The Bolivia Tourism website www.bolivia.travel provides some travel advice and there are countless operators (of differing quality) offering tours including Red Planet Expedition www.redplanetexpedition.com. The Palacio de Sal Hotel can be booked directly through their website www.palaciodesal.com.bo.

309 AMARG
ARIZONA, USA

In the remote Arizona desert is a region known chillingly as 'The Boneyard'. Covering 2,600 acres – an area the size of 1,300 football pitches – The Boneyard is the final resting place of 4,400 military aircraft, standing side by side for as far as the eye can see.

Built in 1946 the 309th Aerospace Maintenance and Regeneration Group (309 AMARG) was constructed next to the Davis-Monthan Air Force Base and became not only the United States' most important military aircraft graveyard, but the world's biggest. Its location is intentionally perfect, chosen for the long-term preservation of these great metal birds and their now decommissioned warheads. The dry, sunny climate minimises corrosion and the region's rock hard sub soil allows the heavy planes and helicopters to be towed and stored with ease.

Many planes come here to die, stripped for their parts, their carcasses left as much-appreciated homes for resident rattlesnakes and scorpions in the hot, dusty desert. Others are sold to allied air forces, getting their second chance to fly again. And hundreds yet stand as a lasting legacy to long decommissioned fleets who were once the elite of military prowess. *F14 Tomcats* stand wing to wing in their dozens alongside *B1 Bombers* and *F4 Phantoms*, long retired after the Vietnam War. Blackhawk helicopters, *F15* and *F16* fighter jets, British Harrier jump jets, *B52 Bombers* and anti-tank *A10 Thunderbolts* – all still in active service – ultimately find their way to 309 AMARG to be disassembled or preserved as part of military heritage.

Despite being an active military base, tours of The Boneyard operate through The Pima Air and Space

Did You Know?

309 AMARG is home to a *Lockheed SR-71 Blackbird*, the fastest air-breathing manned aircraft in the world. Reaching speeds of 2193.2 miles per hour (3529.6 kilometres per hour) – that's 36.55 miles (58.8 kilometres) per minute – the reconnaissance jet is the colour of the night sky, it's aerodynamic shape making it look as though it has just flown out of the movie *Battlestar Galactica*. Despite great advancements in military aviation technology the *Blackbird* has held the record since 1976, and of the 32 aircraft built only 20 still exist today. The oldest in the world is on display at The Pima Air and Space Museum.

Take Me There

How to Visit: One and half hour bus tours of 309 AMARG are arranged through The Pima Air and Space Museum **www.pimaair.org** and are charged in addition to the museum entrance fee. The museum is located 8 miles south of Tucson, Arizona, and is only accessible by car.

Further Information: Discover more about Tucson at **www.visittucson.org** and 309 AMARG at **www.dm.af.mil/units/amarc.asp**.

Museum, one of the largest aviation museums in the world. Begin by spending a few hours exploring the museum's hangars and exhibitions, where 300 aircraft are on display. Immaculately preserved planes from the Korean & Vietnam wars stand alongside the rare *F-107 Ultra Sabre* and the only existing *Martin PBM-5A Mariner* in the world. Visit original Second World War barracks, peer inside a training version of an Apollo space capsule and get up close to President Kennedy's Air Force One before setting off into the dusty graveyard where US$35 billion of pristine military weaponry sit glinting in the Tucson desert.

SERMEQ KUJALLEQ
GREENLAND

Scientists believe that it was one of the vast icebergs which crashed off the tip of the Sermeq Kujalleq glacier that sunk the *Titanic* on her maiden voyage in 1912. Over 100 years on and the world's fastest-moving glacier is moving faster than ever – at a rate of 40 metres (131 feet) per day – shedding great chunks of ice into the frigid seas. In Greenland's remote southwest, the mighty Sermeq Kujalleq is quite literally just the tip of the iceberg (or glacier), the 35 mile (56 kilometre)- long icefjord raging down from the Greenland ice cap.

The statistics are mind-boggling; the glacier calves approximately 35 cubic miles (46 cubic kilometres) of ice annually – the melted equivalent would supply all of the USA's water needs for a year. Some of the icebergs produced by the glacier can be 0.9 cubic miles (1.5 cubic kilometres) in size, the equivalent of 30 football fields. And Greenland's ice cap is the second largest outside of Antarctica – together these two ice caps hold 99% of the world's fresh water.

This polar region, 155 miles (250 kilometres) north of the Arctic Circle, is a fascinating world of gargantuan ice rivers, swirling northern lights and thriving arctic wildlife. It is a protected region, both for its value as a crucial research station for world climate change and for its sheer natural beauty. For 4,400 years people have lived on the shoulder of the vast icefjord, its nutrient-rich waters feeding great schools of halibut and shrimp and fuelling a flourishing fishing economy. Around 4,000 people and 5,000 husky dogs live in the charming little town of Ilulissat, making it Greenland's third largest town, although no roads lead here and, like much of the enormous country, it is accessible only by air and boat.

The edge of the glacier is a short walk from the small town, which perches on the shore of Disko Bay. The surface is strewn with discarded lumps of ice, the crack of white thunder filling the silence as they calve off the glacier. During the summer months the midnight sun turns the ice from a glowing turquoise to an orangey pink, the icebergs resembling great sugary sweets as they float on the water. The cold seas are teeming with life, the vast schools of fish bringing with them seals and Greenland sharks, fin, beluga, minke and occasional blue whales.

Visitors to Ilulissat – whose name quite aptly means 'icebergs' – will find a remote, frosty and stunning wilderness, and a hospitable, modern people immensely proud of their home. Opportunities to get up close to the glacier and icefjord are plentiful; swoop overhead by helicopter, sail into the midnight sun amidst the icebergs, or hike in summer across the face of the icefjord.

Did You Know?

Greenland is the largest island in the world with an area of 1,242,742 square miles (2,000,000 square kilometres). That is bigger than Great Britain, France, Germany, Spain and Italy combined.

Take Me There

How to Visit: Flights go to Greenland's capital Nuuk from Reykjavik, Iceland and Copenhagen, Denmark, and from there on to Ilulissat. Tour companies offer adventure trips details of which can be found on the tourism website.

Further Information: Visit Greenland www.greenland.com has a wealth of travel information to help with planning a trip. For more details on the glacier visit **www.kangia.gl** and **unesco.org**.

CHERNOBYL AND PRIPYAT
UKRAINE

There are dates in history that will forever go down in infamy and 26th April 1986 is one of them. The day started like every other for the residents of Pripyat, most of whom worked in or were relatives of workers in the Chernobyl nuclear power plant on its doorstep. But at 01.23, reactor four suffered a catastrophic power surge that ignited a huge fire sending a plume of radioactive particles into the air. The accident will go down as the worst nuclear disaster on earth, one which saw 50,000 people flee their homes never to return and a death toll that is still being counted almost three decades later.

To grasp the sheer magnitude of the disaster, four hundred times more radioactive material was released from Chernobyl than by the devastating bombing of Hiroshima. The worst hit countries were Belarus, Ukraine and Russia, over 62,137 square miles (100,000 square kilometres) were majorly affected by the fallout and contamination spread across much of Europe. The area around Chernobyl and Pripyat won't be habitable for 20,000 years.

Pripyat wasn't immediately evacuated and daily life carried on as usual; preparations were being made for the May Day funfair, children went to school, and citizens went about their daily lives. The evacuation order didn't arrive until two days later when residents were instructed to take only what they needed for a few days and buses shuttled the 50,000 men, women and children out of the irradiated city – they never returned and most of their belongings remain to this day.

An exclusion zone has been set up 19 miles (30 kilometres) around Chernobyl, and Ukraine now allows strictly monitored tours to enter the area. The number four reactor is encased in a vast concrete sarcophagus but the levels of radiation are still so high it is only possible to view it from 200 metres (656 feet) away. It is a stark and sobering sight as you try and grasp the sheer devastation it caused – predictions are the eventual death toll could reach 4,000.

Entering the ghost city of Pripyat is a chilling experience. Geiger counter in hand you travel through a city unlived in for almost 30 years. Plants and trees have taken over, winding across streets and through buildings in a tangle of overgrown disorder. Smashed windows reveal crumbling schools, apartments and shops littered with Soviet propaganda and possessions that have never been reclaimed; toys, books, and gas masks. In the heart of the apocalyptic town stands the most poignant of all Pripyat's sights, and one which has come to symbolise the devastation; the lonely ferris wheel, destined never to be used and a ghostly and eerie sight to behold.

Did You Know?

A lethal dose of radiation is 500 roentgens over five hours. In some areas of Chernobyl workers received fatal doses in less than a minute, and in the worst hit areas it is estimated there was 20,000 roentgens per hour.

Take Me There

How to Visit: The site is two hours from Kiev and can only be visited as part of an organised tour.

Further Information: There are a number of companies offering tours including Tour Chernobyl **tourchernobyl.com** and Tour Kiev **www.tourkiev.com**. The Ukraine tourism website **www.traveltoukraine.org** offers a good guide to visiting the country.

MOUNT THOR
BAFFIN ISLAND, CANADA

In the far north of the planet, where the arctic circle cuts an invisible slash through an icy, desolate landscape of jagged mountains, unyielding glaciers, and unpassable ice fields, there is one peak that stands out; Mount Thor. In this seemingly interminable wilderness, it rises vertically 1,675 metres (5,495 feet) into the sky, looming as fiercely as its namesake – the great Norse god of thunder – over the Akshayuk Pass below.

Mount Thor is not an easy place to get to. It is located in the Auyuittuq National Park on Baffin Island, one of Canada's remote and gargantuan arctic isles. And it is as far-flung as it is jaw-droppingly impressive. Like a great canine tooth it towers over the ice-free Akshayuk Pass – a travel route long used by the Inuit – through which the Weasel and Owl rivers weave their way beneath the craggy mountains. For 1,250 metres (4,101 feet) the cliff face is an uninterrupted smooth wall of solid granite 15 degrees from vertical which lures rock-climbers and base jumpers in search of ever more daring feats.

All around is a tree-less vista of glacial-carved valleys, tundra and, in the heart of the park, the 3,728 square miles (6000 square kilometres) Penny Ice Cap – a huge expanse of ice and snow – out of which radiate glaciers up to 15 miles (25 kilometres) long. The vegetation is sparse, only the hardiest of mosses and tiny, unlikely wildflowers offering the 12 mammal residents floral nourishment. Lemmings, hares and caribou tiptoe through the park, polar bears pad along the coastal fjords, and Arctic wolves and foxes prowl for scarce food. While land creatures suffer the elements, the polar seas teem with long-toothed walruses, swirling seals, unicorn-headed narwhals and ghostly white beluga whales.

Only the most seasoned of wilderness travellers can make the journey to Mount Thor and the Auyuittuq National Park unguided, the fierce weather putting all who enter at its mercy. Guided expeditions, while still not for the faint-hearted, offer adventure-seekers hiking, skiing on the untouched ice-fields, backcountry camping, dog sledding and wildlife watching. Trek the famous Akshayuk Pass, past great green glacial lakes, 600 metre (2000 feet)-high crashing waterfalls and giant boulders dropped like marbles by retreating glaciers. Kayak the narrow, vertical fjords in search of marine life, or sit, with the northern lights swirling above, and contemplate a place so cold and wild the locals named it Auyuittuq – the land that never melts.

Take Me There

How to Visit: Auyuittuq National Park is remote and only experienced wilderness travellers should venture in unguided (an orientation is mandatory at the Pangnirtung park office). Flights go from Montreal, Ottawa and Yellowknife to Iqaluit and from there on to Pangnirtung. There are several guided expeditions and cruises that venture to this region.

Further Information: The park office in Pangnirtung www.pc.gc.ca should be the main contact for self-guided trips and provide complete packages of trip-planning information. There are a range of expedition companies including Equinox Expeditions www.equinoxexpeditions.com.

Did You Know?

On July 23rd 2006 an American team set the world record for the longest rappel on Mount Thor. Whilst completing the great feat however, a member of the team, Canadian Park Ranger Philip Robinson, tragically fell due to an equipment malfunction and died.

USS ORISKANY
FLORIDA, USA

On 17th May 2006 hundreds watched as thunderous explosions ripped holes in the US aircraft carrier *USS Oriskany*. She sank bow first into the warm waters of the Gulf of Mexico, 22 miles (35 kilometres) off the coast of Pensacola, Florida where she will remain for ever more. But the sinking of the *Oriskany* was no accident that will go down in naval history as a shocking maritime disaster. She is the very first US warship to be intentionally sunk for the purposes of creating an artificial reef – and is today the world's largest.

She is affectionately known as The Great Carrier Reef to the hundreds of scuba divers who delight in exploring her great hull, the top of which is 24 metres (78 feet) below the surface, the bottom at an inaccessible 65 metres (215 feet). At 275 metres (904 feet) long the *Oriskany* is enormous, her island superstructure alone consisting of eight decks. Descending through the clear waters the massive deck comes into view first, the rest of the ship appearing out of the green depths.

The ship had an illustrious past, earning battle stars for her service in both the Korean and Vietnam wars as she plied the Pacific in the 1970s. Tragedy struck in 1966 when one of the worst naval fires since the Second World War broke out aboard, killing 44 servicemen. It was a dark time for the battleship but stories of great bravery emerged in the months that followed. With the end of the Cold War the *Oriskany* was decommissioned and many of her parts are now on display in museums around the country. It wasn't until almost 30 years later that the decision was made that the *Oriskany* would find her forever home just off the Florida coast. In coordination with the Environmental Protection Agency the navy used 230 kilograms (500 pounds) of C4 explosives to sink the great aircraft carrier and create a natural reef for the region's marine life.

Despite her recent arrival to the underwater world the ship has lured a thriving marine life. Groupers and tuna, octopus and barracuda, manta rays and moray eels now call the ship home and, sharks, turtles, dolphins and huge whale sharks make occasional visits. Iridescent tropical fish dart in and out of the captain's bridge and saunter along the vast flight deck where once fighter jets and helicopters roared into the skies. Those that take the plunge find a ship whose proud military history and modern-day environmental role have become intimately entwined.

Did You Know?

At 362 metres (1,187 feet) long, the biggest cruise ship in the world is the *Allure of the Seas* owned by Royal Caribbean (which is just 50 millimetres/2 inches longer than its sister ship). It features an ice-skating rink, 25 restaurants and seven 'neighbourhoods'.

Take Me There

How to Visit: The *USS Oriskany* wreck is located 22 miles (35 kilometres) off Pensacola, Florida and is accessible to certified scuba divers. There are many dive centres offering trips and plenty of accommodation and travel options in Pensacola, Orange Beach and Gulf Shores.

Further Information: Visit Pensacola www.visitpensacola.com offers detailed information on travelling to the area and diving the wreck. There are several dive centres offering trips to the *Oriskany* including Dr Dive www.drdive.com and H2O Below www.ussoriskanydiver.com.

THE DEAD SEA
ISRAEL/JORDAN/WEST BANK

Sitting like a gargantuan oasis in the midst of a dry, dusty cauldron, the Dead Sea is the lowest point on land in the world. Forming a political and physical border between Israel, Jordan and part of the West Bank, the still, warm waters of the lake belie yet another world record – the Dead Sea is also the saltiest body of water on the planet. It is fringed by rocky desert cliffs, red-tinged mountains and profound Biblical sites and its oily, saline water has been sought after for centuries, the therapeutic and restorative properties having created nature's own health and wellness retreat.

At 418 metres (1,312 feet) below sea level, the Dead Sea supports no life. Its waters are 30% salt – nine times more than the oceans. For centuries – indeed since King Herod the Great constructed the cliff top palace today known as Masada on a promontory above the Dead Sea – people have been drawn to the region for its healing tendencies. Skin ailments are eased by bathing in the thick, silky waters bordered by fluffy white salt formations, or from being lathered in the mineral-rich mud that cultivates on the shores.

Biblical history abounds and nature thrives around the Dead Sea which sits in the midst of the great Syrian-African Rift Valley glistening like a dark topaz. Names such as John the Baptist, King David, Queen Cleopatra, Sodom, Gomorrah and Lot are intricately connected with its history and oases such as Ein Gedi provide a lifeline for flora and fauna. In the dry, wild landscape Nubian ibex teeter along impossibly sheer cliffs, hyrax scuttle between the rocks and onager (wild ass) relish in the spring-fed vegetation. Beaches dot the shores of the great lake, great salty caverns pocket the moon-like landscape and camouflaged camels wander the dusty region.

While vast tracts of the Dead Sea coastline are rugged and unspoilt – perfect for bobbing away in the ultra-buoyant water – a few small pockets have been developed into low key, upmarket resorts which host international chain spa facilities. At the other extreme, remote villages and kibbutz offer back-to-nature campsites and eco-friendly activities creating a harmonious combination of bohemian simplicity, Bedouin heritage, trendy resorts, Biblical history and the famed healing powers of the Dead Sea.

Did You Know?

The isolated site of Qumran, perched on the jagged cliffs at the north western end of the Dead Sea, was the site of the discovery of perhaps the world's most significant biblical texts, the Dead Sea Scrolls. Today housed in Jerusalem's Israel Museum, the scrolls are older than any other surviving biblical manuscripts by almost 1,000 years.

Take Me There

How to Visit: Visiting the Dead Sea can be done from both Jordan and Israel. Day trips from Amman, Jerusalem and Tel Aviv are easily organised and there is a wealth of accommodation options including eco-kibbutz, Bedouin camps and upmarket resorts.

Further Information: The official tourism websites for Israel **www.thinkisrael.com** and Jordan **www.visitjordan.com** offer information on visiting the Dead Sea. There are dozens of tours operating daily in both countries including Abraham Tours **www.abrahamtours.com** from Jerusalem, and it is easily visited independently.

BISHOP ROCK
ISLES OF SCILLY, UK

At high tide the Bishop Rock lighthouse seemingly erupts from the surface of the Atlantic Ocean, the waves slapping against the walls of the great beacon. At low tide, there isn't much more to see of this isolated and remote granite outcrop just 46 metres (151 feet) long and 16 metres (52 feet) wide – no bigger than four tennis courts. Here, in the very far southwest of Britain, off Cornwall's craggy coast, Bishop Rock is one of the Isles of Scilly hundreds of mostly uninhabited islands, and the world's smallest island with a building on it.

As Britain's southernmost point, Bishop Rock and it's 46 metre- (151 feet) high lighthouse are at the mercy of the often violent seas, buffeted with powerful, crashing waves. It is a dramatic and remote location, where rare species of seabirds swoop through the fresh air, seal colonies glide through the chilly, clear waters and the sea is littered with the historic wrecks of ships that met their watery ends.

The lighthouse itself is a magnificent tribute to Victorian engineering, built to protect the ships that plied the waters in the 19th century. Construction began in 1847 and despite the difficult and hazardous conditions that plagued workers for a decade, 2,500 tonnes of granite were crafted to create a 35 metre- (115 feet) high lighthouse whose beacon still shines 24 nautical miles across the seas warning mariners of the perilous rocks. The very last keepers left the rock in 1992 when the lighthouse was converted to automatic operation.

Only five of the Isles of Scilly are inhabited, their uncrowded and unspoilt landscapes a mixture of exotic flowers, hardy heathers and wind-sculpted rocks. The summer brings warm weather and the clean waters sparkle a deep turquoise against the little sand beaches. Life is laid-back on the islands, where fresh lobster is served in local eateries and gig-racing (in wooden boats) is a favourite passtime. Nature prevails, and a whole host of activities – cycling, kayaking, scuba diving, sailing, horse-riding and bird-watching – ensure visitors remain outdoors. It is also one of the best places in Britain to experience close encounters with the playful, inquisitive grey seals that swoop through the waters. Organised snorkelling expeditions head out from beautiful St Martin's island. Boat tours to Bishop Rock and its towering lighthouse pass isolated bird sanctuaries and great garrisons which played vital roles in the defeat of the Spanish Armada and both World Wars, before arriving at the tiny rock which stands today as a testament to the power of the sea and a lasting legacy of Britain's maritime heritage.

Take Me There

How to Visit: Boat tours to Bishop Rock run from St Mary's, St Agnes and Bryher islands. Travel to the Isles of Scilly is by plane or ferry from Cornwall. Accommodation includes well-equipped campsites, B&B's and small hotels.

Further Information:

The Isles of Scilly tourism **www.simplyscilly.co.uk** has excellent information on planning a trip, and flights and ferries can be booked through Isles of Scilly Travel **www.islesofscilly-travel. co.uk**. Trips to Bishop Rock can be arranged with Isles of Scilly Boating. Seal snorkelling expeditions are run by Scilly Seal Snorkelling **www.scillysealsnorkelling.com**.

Did You Know?

Folklore has it that the Scilly archipelago may once have been Lyonesse, the lost land of the legendary King Arthur which was swallowed by the sea one terrible night in 1099.

THE NAMIB DESERT
SOUTHERN AFRICA

At first glance, the ancient Namib Desert is a barren and lifeless corner of the planet. The 1,242 mile (2,000 kilometre) expanse of rolling dunes and gravel plains stretching along Africa's south Atlantic coast is almost wholly uninhabited. The great carcasses of ships wrecked on these shores by unforgiving fogs lay in their dozens along the region known notoriously as the Skeleton Coast, and a handful of gold-mining towns remain long abandoned in the harsh and unforgiving terrain.

Yet owing to its antiquity – the desert has existed for 55 million years – the Namib supports one of the world's richest desert ecosystems. Herds of desert-dwelling springbok roam, the cackle of hyenas echo across the dunes and the cold ocean water supports great schools of fish for the colonies of fur seals. Snakes, geckos and rare insects survive the hyper-arid conditions, while further inland in the Namib-Naukluft National Park, Bush elephants, mountain zebras and ostriches roam under the blistering African sun.

Sossusvlei, with its ever-changing, blood-red sand dunes and vivid white clay pans, is a bizarre and fascinating landscape, and an iconic image of Namibia. Great swirling dunes up to 300 metres (984 feet) high – some of the biggest on earth – shift with the times, evolving as they're moulded by the winds that whip off the coast. Here, when the deep orange sun sets it seemingly melts into the dunes, leaving in its wake a rosy pink hue across the scorched land.

Namibia's capital of Windhoek, and the two seaside towns of Swakopmund and Walvia Bay, are the jumping off points for exploring the Namib, and offer a magnitude of desert adventures. Discover the eerie and mysterious fog-clouded beaches of the Skeleton Coast, where sun-parched whale carcasses and rusted ships create a haunting beauty; embark on a wildlife jeep safari in search of Africa's most elusive residents, the rare desert lions; or soar over the great dunes in a light plane or hot air balloon and watch as the sand is whipped off their summits like candyfloss. Far from a land of ghosts, the Namib is an ancient yet ever-changing landscape whose residents have battled, and succeeded, to survive for millennia despite the harshest of environments.

Did You Know?

'The Skeleton Coast' was the name of John Henry Marsh's book chronicling the shipwrecking of the *MV Dunedin Star* and has become the accepted name for the region. Carrying passengers and Second World War supplies to South Africa in 1942, the British ship ran aground. There were 42 people and crew who managed to get ashore, yet rescue efforts were blighted by the unforgiving conditions. Over the 24 days it took to affect a rescue many rescuers lost their lives when another ship ran aground and an aircraft crashed into the stormy seas.

Take Me There

How to Visit: Jeep safaris and scenic flights to the Skeleton Coast, Namib-Naukluft National Park and Sossuvlei (as well as other desert adventure activities) can be arranged from Windhoek, Swakopmund and Walvis Bay. International flights arrive in Windhoek International Airport. For Sossuvlei, Sesriem is the starting point where there are luxury lodges, desert homesteads or back-to-nature campsites.

Further Information: Contact the Namibia Tourism Authority www.namibiatourism.com.na and Namibia Wildlife Resorts www.nwr.com.na for further information on visiting, accommodation options and activities.

ILHA GRANDE
BRAZIL

At first glance Ilha Grande appears to be just another beautiful tropical island. Palm trees sway in the breeze, thatched roof buildings offer succulent seafood meals, and there is mile upon mile of white sand beaches. But Ilha Grande is no ordinary sun, sea and surf destination. It is a place where Magellanic penguins meet tropical rainforests and Southern Right whales can be seen on coral reefs. It is a place whose dark history as a pirate hideaway, leper colony and high security prison are barely believable but for their remains enshrouded in the dense rainforest. And with the exception of the local fire engine, lone police car and a single refuse truck there are no vehicles at all on the 120 square miles (193 square kilometre)-sized island.

There is nothing but the crashing of Atlantic waves to interrupt the screeching calls of the howler monkeys or the live samba music pumped out by the low-key bars in the island's main village, Vila do Abraão. It is a refreshingly slow-paced destination, where if you want to explore hard-to-find beaches and hidden waterfalls then you'll have to walk to them – in fact, anywhere you want to go entails a hike or boat ride. It is a model for eco-tourism and nature conservation, the largely undeveloped land left rugged and pristine for the enjoyment of its abundant wildlife not the comforts of its visitors. Yet it's this wildness that is Ilha Grande's true charm. It's rich ecosystem of thick Atlantic rainforest and tropical reefs are paradise homes to monkeys and sloths, schools of fish and inquisitive turtles. Around 93 miles (150 kilometres) of hiking trails weave through the island past waterfalls and mountain peaks before emerging onto fine white sand beaches dotted with ramshackle huts. The most famous of them all is Lopes Mendes beach, whose wild beauty and rolling waves have seen it contend for the crown of Brazil's most picturesque.

Small scale eco-tourism has made a slow appearance in the last 20 years, and in pretty little Abraão, low-rise pousadas (hotels), rustic bars and restaurants huddle together in the cobbled streets under fronds of banana, jackfruit and palm trees. Eco-lodges are in their element, offering visitors the chance to while away their days snorkelling, hiking, kayaking, practicing yoga or simply swinging lazily in hammocks. There are no roads outside of the main village – why would there be? Yet Ilha Grande is no time warp to a period before the advent of cars. It is a natural haven that has chosen to forgo the luxuries of powered travel and let the island dictate the pace of life.

Did You Know?

Right whales are the rarest of all large whales. They got their fateful name from whalers who considered them the 'right' whale to hunt for their slow swimming speeds and thick oily blubber. The rarest of all whales is the highly elusive spade-toothed beaked whale. Only a few specimens have ever been found intact and none have ever been seen alive.

Take Me There

How to Visit: From Rio de Janeiro public transport leads to Angra dos Reis from where ferries leave for Ilha Grande. There are a number of hostels, pousadas (hotels) and a handful of resorts on the island.

Further Information: For help planning a trip to Brazil the official tourism website **www.visitbrasil.com** has lots of information. Resorts and pousadas on Ilha Grande include Asalem **www.asalem.com.br** and The Island Experience **www.theislandexperience.com**.

TRISTAN DA CUNHA
SOUTH ATLANTIC OCEAN

Shrouded in cloud and with the navy blue, white-capped ocean stretching in every direction as far as the eye can see, the archipelago of Tristan Da Cunha is an undoubtedly isolated place. Its closest neighbours are St Helena, 1,510 miles (2,430 kilometres) to the north, and the coast of South Africa 1,740 miles (2,800 kilometres) to the east. In the true heart of the southern Atlantic Ocean, this tiny group of islands and the 275 people who call it home are at the mercy of not only the weather and isolation – there is no airport and no ferries ply these waters – but the active volcano that towers above Edinburgh of the Seven Seas, the only town.

Yet life in the world's most remote inhabited place holds a certain romance about it. Crime is unheard of and unemployment non-existent – fishing for crayfish and farming sustains the 80 families. A sense of wild freedom prevails in the rugged landscape, there are strong family bonds and a distinct air of yesteryear emanates.

Despite its geographical distance, Tristan Da Cunha's green fields dotted with sheep, its great potato patches, and its wet, cloudy climate echo images of Great Britain, who formally annexed the islands in 1816 to ensure the French could not rescue Napoleon Bonaparte from his prison in 'nearby' St Helena. Indeed, English is the native tongue, albeit a unique dialect infused with old English, Afrikaans, Italian and early Americanisms – evidence of the island's heritage.

Tristan Da Cunha is the only inhabited island within the small archipelago, its neighbouring islands, the wonderfully-named Inaccessible, Nightingale, Middle, Stoltenhoff and Gough, being home only to great colonies of birds, including the elaborately-crested Rockhopper penguin. On Tristan's 25 miles (40 kilometres) of storm-bashed coastline, basalt cliffs rise 600 metres (1968 feet) high and the interior – a mere 47 miles (76 kilometres) square – is predominantly mountainous and snow-covered in winter. The clearest of streams pour through the shallow valleys and albatross' soar in the skies above.

Adventure cruises make land here as they ply the southern Atlantic waters down to Antarctica, the vast majority of visitors arriving this way. Yet for the truly intrepid, booking a passage aboard a fishing boat from Cape Town is a choppy journey not for the faint-hearted. Getting to Tristan Da Cunha is most certainly an adventure in itself, the world's most remote island fully living up to its accolade.

Did You Know?

The islands of Gough and Inaccessible are designated nature reserves and an UNESCO World Heritage Site often considered a contender for the most important seabird colony in the world. 54 species have been recorded here and of these, four are threatened and three are endemic. Almost half of the world's Rockhopper penguins come here to nest.

Take Me There

How to Visit: Tristan Da Cunha can be visited as part of cruises taking in the southern Atlantic islands and/or Antarctica. Alternatively, there are infrequent fishing vessels carrying up to 12 passengers departing from Cape Town, South Africa. Permission must be sought from the island council and passages are booked up to a year in advance.

Further Information: The best source of information is the official guide published by the Tristan Da Cunha Government **www.tristandc.com**. Various companies offer cruises including Oceanwide Expeditions **www.oceanwide-expeditions.com**.

THE SMITHSONIAN INSTITUTION
WASHINGTON DC, USA

To comprehend the sheer enormity of Washington DC's Smithsonian Institution, consider this: if you spent just one minute looking at every single item in the museums' collections, after 10 years (with no sleep) you'd only have laid eyes on about a quarter. The complex is simply vast, a magnificent, fascinating and at times quirky treasure trove of all things American, awarding it the nickname 'America's attic'. Some 137 million items are packed into 19 different museums, research centres and even a zoo – making this not only the world's largest museum complex but America's richest and most valuable national heritage.

The Smithsonian is 165 years old, and came to being when a wealthy British scientist bequeathed his fortune to the 'establishment for the increase and diffusion of knowledge among men' – mysterious because he had never once visited America. Since those early days it has grown to include the titans, the Air and Space Museum, the Natural History Museum and the Museum of American History. Their iconic exhibits draw crowds of millions, from the original Star-Spangled Banner to the Apollo 11 lunar landing module, the Wright brothers' 1903 Flyer, and Dorothy's red slippers from the classic movie *The Wizard of Oz*.

Even with the majority of the museums lining the National Mall, trying to visit more than one or two in any given day is a herculean task. Ambling through the exhibits reveals 3.5 billion year old fossils and prehistoric dinosaurs (there's even some Jurassic poop), the 45-carat Hope Diamond, an Air France Concorde and the Gunboat Philadelphia, the U.S. Navy's oldest surviving war vessel. Gaze with envy at the gowns worn by the 'First Ladies', come face to face with the presidents of centuries past in the National Portrait Gallery, and realise how far technology has come when you find Alexander Graham Bell's 1876 telephone. From prehistoric great white sharks to Tony Hawk's first skateboard the range is staggering and enthralling – there's even the slightly macabre top hat President Lincoln was wearing when he was assassinated.

The variety of the museums and their eclectic exhibits see visitors leave educationally-saturated yet equally frustrated at barely having scratched the surface of what's on offer. There are IMAX films and planetarium shows to watch, flight simulators to try and quiet contemplation to be found in the galleries of modern and contemporary art from America, Africa and Asia. From an insect zoo to the national zoo, and from American Indian heritage to the Declaration of Independence the Smithsonian Institute is undoubtedly the star-spangled museum of America.

Did You Know?

The Air and Space Museum is home to the *Bell X-1* airplane which was the first to fly faster than the speed of sound in 1947 – it reached speeds of 700 miles (1,127 kilometres) per hour and Mach 1.6. It was named *Glamorous Glennis* after pilot Capt. Charles E. 'Chuck' Yeager's wife.

Take Me There

How to Visit: There is good public transport to all the city's museums from around Washington DC. Admission to all museums is free.

Further Information: There are individual websites for all 19 museums and the zoo but a good first resource is the Smithsonian main website **www.si.edu**. For help on planning a trip to Washington DC visit **www.washington.org**.

THE NGORONGORO CRATER
TANZANIA

Two to three million years ago, in the heart of Africa's Great Rift Valley, a volcano so large it eclipsed even the mighty Mount Kilimanjaro exploded with such ferocity that it collapsed in on itself, creating a vast crater known as a caldera. It is 12 miles (19 kilometres) wide, a dormant and perfectly formed giant bowl of wilderness 102 square miles (264 square kilometres) in size in which 25,000 animals roam in nature's very own reserve.

It is often dubbed Africa's Garden of Eden, for wildlife wanders the Ngorongoro Crater in numbers few other places on the great continent can rival. In the flat basin, acacia trees provide shade from the hot African sun, black rhinos, wildebeest, zebras, eland, gazelles, reedbucks and warthogs graze on the savannahs and grasslands. In their midst the predators are spoilt for choice, cheetahs, leopards and hyenas never short of an easy meal, while lions laze in the short grasses in close-knit prides in what is the densest population in the world. Further up the 610 metre (2001 feet)-high crater rim, monkeys, baboons, elephants, buffalo and jackals take shelter in the thick montane forests.

A micro-world of landscapes has formed like a perfect African snow globe penned in by the volcanic walls of the crater. The rains bring life to this hot yet fertile cauldron, and streams wind their way from the upland forests through open moorland and sprawling grasslands to feed lakes and swamps inhabited by lumbering hippos. The flamingo-filled Lake Magadi dominates the basin floor providing a lifeline to both the wildlife and indigenous Maasai who graze their cattle on the lower slopes. The possibility of seeing the Big 5 – the African buffalo, rare black rhino, elephant, lion and leopard – is one of the park's great draws and safaris often herald sightings of all. Yet the most incredible sight is undoubtedly the great wildebeest migration. Come December, 1.7 million wildebeest, 470,000 gazelles and 260,000 zebras thunder across the Serengeti Plains on their route south, returning a few months later in June.

Safari lodges dot the perimeter of the gated crater park in a mixture of new and old, many dating to the 1930s and 40s when Europeans first started travelling to Ngorongoro. Green lawns mowed by grazing zebras stretch out before them and, as night falls, the air fills with the sounds of nature's calls.

Did You Know?

Within the Ngorongoro Conservation Area is a steep-sided ravine called Olduvai Gorge, one of the most prehistoric sites ever discovered. It was at Olduvai that the earliest known human specimens in the world were found which cemented our understanding of human evolution.

Take Me There

How to Visit: Many visit as part of a safari tour including the Serengeti, and there are many national and international operators. The town of Arusha is the gateway to the crater which can be accessed from Kilimanjaro International Airport or Nairobi Airport, Kenya. 4x4 vehicles will take you from Arusha into the crater. There are many hotels and lodges in the vicinity.

Further Information: The Ngorongoro Conservation Area **www.ngorongorocrater.org** is a good source of travelling planning information, and UNESCO **whc.unesco.org** offers more background on the ecology, culture and conservation of the region.

MONACO

Nowhere in the world epitomises glamour and affluence quite like Monaco. The world's second smallest country – only the Vatican City is smaller – measures just 0.78 square miles (2.02 square kilometres), a tiny blip of land perched on the French Riviera steeped in royal history and visited by the world's glitterati. A total 36,371 people are shoe-horned into the country – that would be 43,000 people per square mile – a mix of international celebrities and millionaires, French nationals and a scattering of locally-born Monegasques, making this the world's most densely inhabited country. With residents living to an average 90 years Monaco also takes the crown for the world's highest life expectancy.

Monaco is a principality whose very existence is intricately entwined with the royal family who govern it. Since 1297 the Grimaldi family have controlled the minute city-state, the opulent Palais Princier (Prince's Palace) standing proudly over its land. The reigning monarch Prince Albert II is the son of Prince Rainier III who famously married American film star Grace Kelly in 1956, her old-school glamour evoking a true sense of fairy-tale romance. Princess Grace died in a car accident in 1982 and she is remembered lovingly throughout the country, from the perfumed beauty of the Princess Grace Rose Garden in Fontvielle Park, to Avenue Princess Grace in the heart of vibrant Monte Carlo district, and her final resting place in the white stone Monaco Cathedral.

Everything about Monaco screams extravagance, the little bubble of luxury oozing wealth and ostentation. Designer shops and haute couture boutiques line the streets, great superyachts, each bigger than the next, squeeze into Port Hercule, and flashy cars hum around the narrow steep roads. It is a playground for the rich and famous, from the lavish Monaco Opera House and Casino, with its grand atrium, dancing fountains, sculptures and tuxedoed patrons to the chandeliered hotels and Michelin restaurants. Once a year Formula One comes to town, the race track snaking through the city and along the seafront district of La Condamine, filling the air with an excited charge and the scream of race cars.

Despite the glitz and glamour Monaco has managed to retain a sense of serenity and history. Narrow alleyways weave through the picturesque old town of Monaco-Ville, where churches, squares and the great palace sit quietly away from the hubbub surrounding it. Immaculate manicured gardens cover 250,000 square metres (820,210 square feet) of the country and countless museums provide a dash of cultural learning, most notably the Oceanographic Museum. Monaco is a beguiling place, one that revels in its status as one of the most exuberant and exclusive places on the planet, a tiny stretch of land with an enormous personality.

Did You Know?

James Bond is a particular fan of Monaco and has visited the casino in *Never Say Never Again*, *GoldenEye* and *Casino Royale*. James Bond actor Sir Roger Moore is one of Monaco's long-time residents.

Take Me There

How to Visit: Monaco doesn't have its own international airport but is served by the Nice Côte d'Azur International Airport 11 miles (18 kilometres) away. There are excellent road and rail links connecting the two and plenty of high end accommodation.

Further Information: Both www.visitmonaco.com and www.monte-carlo.mc offer detailed travel information.

MOUNT STROMBOLI
ITALY

Rising out of Italy's deep blue Tyrrhenian Sea, Mount Stromboli is as perfect as volcanoes come. Towering 924 metres (3,031 feet) above sea level – and an even further 1000 metres (3,280 feet) below it – the volcano engulfs the entire island, a perfect cone bursting skywards from the ocean's surface, a trail of smoke drifting from its summit. It is an image that has played out for centuries, for Mount Stromboli has been erupting continuously for over 2,000 years.

Bursting glowing rocks of lava up to 200 metres (656 feet) above its craters every two to three hours has awarded Mount Stromboli the nickname 'The Lighthouse of the Mediterranean', and against the backdrop of the black, starry night sky it is one of nature's most magnificent shows. Small eruptions are constant, yet major eruptions give little warning, and explode with unforgiving ferocity wreaking havoc on the houses of the few hundred faithful residents that call it home. Despite recent eruptions in 2003 and 2007 Stromboli's loyal residents choose to stay, finding a certain charm and rugged beauty in living with one of nature's greatest and most volatile beasts.

Only two fishing villages exist on the remotest of the Aeolian islands, separated from one another by the Sciara del Fuoco (Street of Fire), down which lava and rocks ocassionally tumble to the sea. Picturesque white-washed houses cluster above the unspoiled black sand beaches, the little lanes – travelled only by donkey and scooter – are lined with cacti and wildflowers, and a slow, traditional Mediterranean pace of life remains. Despite the fierce power of the volcano looming over the island spurting molten lava into the air with each great cough, an air of romanticism envelopes Stromboli. A handful of tiny restaurants serve rustic Sicilian dishes and fishing boats trundle in and out of port. Ingrid Bergman's scandalous love affair with director Roberto Rossellini unfolded on Stromboli's shores, and Dolce and Gabanna even have a holiday home here.

There are no airports and no cars to spoil Stromboli's rugged beauty and timeless charm. Boats shuttle visitors in and out of the small harbour from the Sicilian town of Milazzo, and guided evening hikes up the volcano reward the adventurous with a night spent watching over the rumblings of the great crater. On nights when explosive firework spectacles of molten lava pour down the mountainside, boat trips into the harbour offer a truly spectacular show.

Did You Know?

Mount Vesuvius, located a stone's throw from Naples, Italy is the only active volcano on mainland Europe and is considered one of the world's most dangerous. In AD 79 it decimated the towns of Pompeii and Herculaneum, perfectly preserving them beneath a layer of lava. Today they are some of the most important Roman archaeological sites in the world.

Take Me There

How to Visit: You can only get to Stromboli by boat and the main Sicilian port for the Aeolians is Milazzo. Guided tours up the volcano begin in the evening and return at sunrise.

Further Information: There are several tour companies offering volcano treks including Magma Trek **www.magmatrek.it**. Both Italy's official tourism website **www.italia.it** and UNESCO **whc.unesco.org** are good sources of information on the Aeolian Islands.

GREAT MOSQUE OF DJENNÉ
MALI

From a distance the Great Mosque of Djenné looks like a giant sandcastle, its brown turrets towering above the little brown city in the heart of which it stands. A sandcastle is in fact not that far from reality, for this desert-dwelling city is made from mud, its buildings seemingly erupting from the ground like a camouflaged oasis in the middle of Mali's remote landscape. The Great Mosque is the grandest of them all, a living part of the city which stands as the world's largest mud building.

Djenné is one of sub-Saharan Africa's oldest cities, once a marketplace for merchants trading gold in and out of Timbuktu. During the Middle Ages it became one of the world centres of Islamic scholarship and thousands arrived to study in the madrassas (schools). While various mosques have stood in the centre of Djenné over the centuries, the current one owes its origins to the French colonialists. In 1906 and under the direction of the city's guild of masons, they built a mosque whose influences and architectural style have made it one of Africa's most famous landmarks.

The mosque is both the geographic and spiritual heart of Djenné, standing on a raised platform to guard against the waters of the Bani River that wraps itself around the city. All around it the mud buildings reflect the centuries of traditions and craftsmanship, their sun-baked earth bricks held together by sand and earth and plastered with yet more mud. The mosque too is made entirely of adobe and its cone shaped minarets are topped with ostrich eggs. Beams of palm poke out of its walls – which act both as supports and natural scaffolding – and electricity has been shunned in order to retain the historical authenticity. On its doorstep the weekly market erupts in a swirl of pungent spicy scents, colourful textiles and bleating goats.

Djenné is a world away from the bustle of other African cities, and a charm of yesteryear pervades the narrow streets wandered by donkeys and chickens. Its residents take shelter from the blistering African sun in the doorways of their mud-built houses, clothed in brightly coloured traditional robes, and a lively annual festival sees thousands of residents come together to repair the mosque that sits in their midst.

The city is a fascinating place to visit, steeped in religious and artisanal traditions and with a proud indigenous heritage. However due to a risqué fashion shoot held inside the mosque in 1996 which outraged the devout locals, non-Muslims are no longer allowed to enter.

Did You Know?

Djenné's Great Mosque might hold the world record for the largest mud building but the largest mud city can be found in Peru. The city of Chan Chan was built in 850 AD and is 12.4 square miles (20 square kilometres) in size.

Take Me There

How to Visit: Djenné is on the road that leads from the capital of Bamako to the large town of Mopti in the north and there is public transport running between the two. There are a handful of hotels and hostels of traditional mud brick style.

Further Information: UNESCO whc.unesco.org offers detailed information on the mud buildings of Djenné. There are several accommodation options including the charming Hotel Djenné Djenno **www.hoteldjennedjenno.com.**

DAINTREE
QUEENSLAND, AUSTRALIA

Over 140 million years ago, the red, dusty desert that is home to Australia's iconic Ayers Rock was blanketed by a thick tropical rainforest. The climate was warm, humid and the rains fell in abundance, feeding the lush jungle and the abounding life it supported. Today that ancient jungle has all but disappeared, all except for a last, vast remaining tract of rainforest known as Daintree.

In Queensland's northernmost stretches, Daintree Rainforest tumbles all the way down to empty sandy white beaches, fringed by crystal clear waters and the world's largest coral reef, the Great Barrier Reef. Forest-clad mountains, waterfalls, deep gorges, and fast flowing streams are home to rare and primitive plants and wildlife, and a proud indigenous heritage prevails. Its ecosystem is one of the most ancient and complex on earth, a land where prehistoric crocodiles saunter silently along the rivers and mangroves, where kangaroos live in trees, and where the planet's biggest concentration of primitive flowering plants flourish. It is home to a third of Australia's mammals and half of its bird species including the endangered, six foot-tall cassowary.

Amidst the grandeur of Australia's largest rainforest, the landscape is as varied as its exotic inhabitants.

Cape Tribulation's semi-circle of hills enclose the glinting blue sea in their midst, forming a grand natural amphitheatre. To its west, Mount Pieter Botte and its towering granite outcrops overlook the forest below, and the settlements of Daintree Village and Mossman – settled by timber cutters in the 19th century – are home to sugar cane and tropical fruit farms in the sweeping valleys.

The region is a playground for back-to-nature experiences and eco-tourism activities. It has a relaxed and bohemian vibe where visitors can climb into the rainforest canopy for a bird's eye view across the Great Barrier Reef, swish high through the forest on a cable, snorkel the clear waters of Mossman River and gorge, or drive the 4-wheel-drive Bloomfield Track. After a night spent in a luxurious eco-spa, traditional farm-stay or tree-top cabin, head off into an ancient living jungle and fish for barramundi on the River Daintree, discover remote islands and coral cays by kayak, take a guided ecology tour into the mangroves, beach-comb tranquil sandy coves or hike amidst Aboriginal lands.

Did You Know?

Stretching for over 1,615 miles (2,600 kilometres) – and visible from Outer Space – the Great Barrier Reef is the world's largest coral reef. It is made up of 2,900 individual reefs, 900 islands and is the size of Germany. One tenth of the planet's total fish species can be found living with the reef system.

Take Me There

How to Visit: Port Douglas, located a short distance from Cairns, is the jumping off point to the region. Accommodation ranges from hotels to B&B's, farm-stays, campsites, eco-retreats and backpacker options. Rainforest tours and activities can be arranged from Port Douglas, Daintree or Mossman.

Further Information: The Queensland tourism **www.experiencequeensland.com** and Tourism Port Douglas and Daintree websites **www.destinationdaintree.com** contain detailed travel guides to the region.

THE AMERICAN QUEEN
MISSISSIPPI, USA

The largest steamboat ever built, the grand and opulent American Queen, stands as a magnificent expression of a bygone era. Plying the mighty rivers of the Old South she evokes memories of the regal steamers of the 19th century, her Victorian grandeur as inviting as the Antebellum architecture of the mansions on which she was designed. As her great paddlewheel churns and eddies in the deep waters of the Mississippi and Ohio rivers she floats past the ever-changing scenery of America's heartland, the sweet scent of magnolia trees and the sounds of Jazz, ragtime and bluegrass filling the air. It is a timeless and romantic way to travel, a journey of discovery along Old Man River and her soulful history.

Adorned with antiques and a décor of Victorian charm, 222 elegant staterooms accommodate 436 passengers, their French doors opening onto six decks of lacy filigree patterns and ornamental woodwork. In honour of the great author who began his world wanderings from his home in Hannibal, Missouri, the Mark Twain library is a treasure trove of 1800s river travel, the polished wood and Tiffany lamps creating an ambience of old-fashioned southern luxury. Within the two-deck-high Grand Saloon, menus reflect the beloved cuisine of the Deep South. Designed by acclaimed American chef Regina Charboneau, the meals honour the region's Creole and Cajun flavours, where sugary beignets, corn and shrimp fritters and glazed pork loin are served.

The dark waters of the Mighty Mississippi have long been the blood line of the south, great cities and small towns lining its shores telling the stories of Native Indians, pioneers and Civil War, a time when the north and south were divided by this very water. In its lower reaches, the spirited cities of New Orleans and Memphis, with their old-school charisma and musical legacy, are separated by great cotton plantations, blossoming gardens and dense woodlands. In its upper reaches, the modern, artsy cities of St. Louis, Minneapolis and St. Paul are steeped in tales of French fur traders and frontier battles, engulfed amidst the pristine landscape where Mark Twain's Tom Sawyer and Huckleberry Finn once roamed. Wildlife, from wolves to bald eagles, ramble through the rolling hills of Wisconsin and Minnesota as the American Queen sweeps her way along the Ohio River's Great Plains, where tales of Davy Crockett come to life and wild salmon wind their way upstream.

Did You Know?

Graceland is one of America's most famous homes, bought by Elvis Presley in 1957. The colonial style mansion, with its iconic Music Gates, was The King's rock 'n roll home for 20 years and is his final resting place. Over 600,000 fans make the pilgrimage to Graceland every year, making it the second most visited private house in the Unites States after the White House.

Take Me There

How to Visit: The American Queen is run by the American Steamboat Company and offers 9-day themed cruises throughout the lower and upper Mississippi River and Ohio and Tennessee starting in several of the port towns.

Further Information: The American Steamboat Company website **www.americanqueensteamboatcompany.com** lists full itineraries for the year ahead as well as a detailed brochure which can be ordered. Further information on visiting Graceland can be found at **www.graceland.com**.

DALLOL
ETHIOPIA

In 1913, in California's Mojave Desert, Death Valley National Park recorded a skin blistering temperature of 57°C (134°F), the hottest ever measured. While this mercury-topping place might hold the world's most extreme temperature, the highest annual temperature – with a year-round average of 35°C (96°F) – is found in a scorching cauldron of sizzling land in the heart of Africa in a place called Dallol, Ethiopia.

Dallol is one of the most truly remote places on the planet. The great collapsed volcano – the only one in the world to have a crater below sea level – sits in the midst of the Danakil Depression. It is a vast hydrothermal field where the blazing heat comes from the skies above and the bubbling ground below in one of the world's most volcanic regions. There are few places on the surface of the planet that create more of an assault on the body. Raging temperatures combine with over 60% humidity and blazing sandstorms. Lakes of potent acid run under fierce-looking salt formations, and active volcanoes and shuddering earthquakes cause lava to bubble up from the centre of the earth. Only the local Afar people and their camels live in this terrifying region where average temperature highs are 41°C (105.8°F) soaring to over 46.4°C (115.6°F).

From the blistering heat to the toxic pools of mustard-yellow, neon-green and alarming purple – and the need for armed guards to accompany the few extreme adventurists who venture here – there is no doubt that Dallol is extreme. Yet it is also one of the most bizarrely beautiful places imaginable, a fantastical land of psychedelic colours, bubbling hot springs, and steaming geysers. Multi-coloured and surreal, the salt formations resemble giant lumps of coral or strange toadstools, others looking more like egg shells of jagged crust, and a smell of sulphur cloaks the region. The Erta Ale volcano stretches 18 miles (30 kilometres) wide, its lava-filled lake bubbling red hot.

Only the hardiest of travellers make their way to Dallol, a scattering of heavily-armed tours running from the town of Mekele into the sands of the desert and on to the salt flats before arriving at Dallol. Six- to ten-day jeep and camel tours venture into the region offering you the chance to stay in the tiny Afar village of Hamed-Ela, camp on the volcano and stare across an alien landscape. Embarking into this sweltering pocket of Africa you will pass great camel caravans weighed down under blocks of salt mined by the local tribespeople, eat freshly slaughtered goat under starry skies and camp on the volcano rim as its molten core bubbles beneath you.

Did You Know?

It is widely believed that coffee originated in the Ethiopian province of Kaffa. Legend has it that a goatherder noticed his goats didn't sleep after eating certain berries and tried them for himself only to discover the energising properties.

Take Me There

How to Visit: Dallol is a harsh and volatile no man's land and you can only visit by armed tours. Flights from the capital Addis Ababa go to Mekele which is the jumping off point to the Danakil region.

Further Information: A handful of companies begin tours in Mekele including:
Ethiopian Travel Tours **www.ethiopiatraveltours.com**,
African Adventure Tours **www.african-adventure-tours.com**
and Aberus Ethiopia Tours **www.aberusethiopiatours.com**.

SAN ALFONSO DEL MAR
CHILE

The world's largest swimming pool could easily be mistaken for the world's smallest sea, or at the very least the world's largest lagoon. To dive in and swim from one end to the other would be a herculean feat of physical prowess, for it measures a kilometre in length – that's 20 Olympic-size swimming pools end to end. Located along Chile's Pacific coast near the city of Algarrobo, and a short distance from the capital of Santiago, the 8 hectare, 250,000 cubic metre (66 million gallon) swimming pool is the largest navigable man-made lagoon in the world.

Small dinghies and their colourful sails flit across the surface of the iridescent blue water, kayaks glide past powdery white sand beaches and bubbles plop to the surface from scuba lessons below. For the San Alfonso del Mar complex is a place of leisure and relaxation, a place where palm trees sway, Jacuzzi baths gurgle and cascades trickle. The lagoon's azure colour rivals that of any tropical paradise, the crystal clear salt-water glimmering like a great topaz at the heart of the building complex, just a stone's throw from the crashing waters of the Pacific and the 1.2 miles- (2 kilometre) long windswept expanse of beach.

The gargantuan body of water is solar powered to a balmy 26°C (78°F), 9°C (48°F) warmer than the sea water that it draws in for filtration from the Algarrobo beach. The computer-controlled suction and filtration system is state of the art, using ten times less water than a golf course, 100 times fewer chemicals than traditional disinfection and drinking water systems, and only 2% of the energy required by conventional filtering technologies. With no motorised water craft permitted on the lagoon to spoil the tranquillity a green ethos prevails in this man-made Atlantis.

With the great pool at its heart, 1,300 apartments and a mini city of luxury facilities make up the colossal complex which is a favourite with holidaying Chileans. From beauty spas to cinemas, exhibition galleries to restaurants, and gyms to nightclubs it is a resort built to entertain. On the shore of the lagoon a shimmering glass pyramid encases South America's only indoor beach – complete with swaying palm trees, heated sand and jet-water massage beds – while the country's largest aquarium introduces visitors to 42 different species of Chile's marine life.

Did You Know?

At 34.5 metres (113 feet) deep, Nemo 33 in Brussels, Belgium is the deepest swimming pool in the world. It contains 2,500,000 litres (550,000 gallons) of un-chlorinated water and a series of caves. making it also the world's only scuba diving adventure park.

Take Me There

How to Visit: The 1,300 apartments in the San Alfonso del Mar are privately-owned holiday homes but many are available to rent through the central booking office. The resort is located 56 miles (90 kilometres) from Santiago de Chile and accessible via good road links and public transport.

Further Information: The apartments can be booked through the San Alfonso del Mar booking office: www.sanalfonso.cl. The official tourism website www.chile.travel is a good source of information on visiting Chile.

THE MALDIVES

A ribbon of tiny, sand-ringed coral atolls swirls through the heart of the Indian Ocean, it's warm, Vodka-clear waters home to a dazzling array of tropical marine life. They are mere blips above the surface of the gently shimmering sea. Together these 1,200 – mostly uninhabited – islands spread over 56,000 square miles (90,000 square kilometres) forming one of the world's most geographically diverse nations and, with an average elevation of just 1.8 metres (5 feet 10 inches), the planet's lowest country.

The Maldives evoke a sense of tropical perfection few other places can compete with. Sitting atop a vast ridge which runs 596 miles (960 kilometres) beneath the ocean, the miniscule islets are home to world famous luxury resorts, their stilted, palm-thatched bungalows jutting enticingly into the sea, promising honeymooners and sun-worshippers opulence and staggering natural beauty far from the crowds.

The Maldives have long stood on the trading routes of the Indian Ocean, giving them a varied and colourful culture full of world influences, which varies from one island to another. Local music has an essence of African drumming; traditional Maldivian sailboats known as dhoni's resemble the Arabian dhows; and the fine architecture seen on the country's ancient mosques has retained the flavour of Southeast Asia.

To add to its list of paradise-enhancing accolades the Maldives are also one of the world's best scuba diving and snorkelling destinations. Powdery white sand beaches overhung with palm trees which sway lazily in the warm breeze give way to a thriving underwater world. Clear, tepid lagoons harbour juvenile fish which dart through the corals; sharks, turtles and manta rays soar along the great walls which drop into the deep blue; and gentle whale sharks – the world's largest fish – sashay slowly by.

For the most part the Maldives is an undoubtedly upmarket destination, a glamorous yet tranquil haven, where the luxury is provided as much by the abounding natural beauty as by the five star resorts who set the standards for tropical holidays. For the independent visitor however, a proud cultural heritage, a long history and a genuine sense of local hospitality – coupled with charming guesthouses and a wide ferry network – make the Maldives one of the planet's most alluring, back-to-nature destinations.

Did You Know?

At such low elevation, the Maldives are under huge threat from rising sea levels, and it is possible that most of the island nation could be submerged by the end of the century. The country's president announced plans to buy land in India, Sri Lanka or Australia as a safe guard against the rising water levels. If the 300,000 people of the Maldives moved elsewhere it would be the first country on the planet forced to abandon its homeland because of global warming.

Take Me There

How to Visit: Flights to the Maldives land at the Mahle International Airport from where ferries or float planes shuttle visitors to other islands. Resorts can be booked directly or through tour operators, and for independent visitors there is a ferry network and independently-run guesthouses.

Further Information: The Maldives Tourism website www.visitmaldives.com is a good source of information on the history and culture of the country as well as providing practical travel tips. It has a comprehensive list of accommodation options.

THE MUSA UNDERWATER MUSEUM
CANCUN, MEXICO

From the air a dark shadow gently ripples below Mexico's turquoise waters, in stark contrast to the fine white sand and colourful reef that dazzles against the year-round sunshine. Slip beneath the surface of the Caribbean water however, and the shadows come to life as a 500-strong collection of figures stand in unison, an eerie and beautiful underwater sculpture garden that is slowly melting into the natural landscape and providing a much-needed artificial reef for the marine life of the region.

Mexico's Cancun has long been one of the country's top destinations, luring visitors with its balmy weather, mile upon mile of sand beaches and fiesta atmosphere. Yet the pressures of tourism, as well as the ravages of numerous violent hurricanes, have taken their toll on the sub-aquatic environment – indeed, 750,000 people visit the Cancun-Isla Mujeres Marine Park each year, making it one of the most visited stretches of water in the world. In 2009 British sculptor Jason deCaires Taylor, along with five Mexican sculptors and support from the National Marine Park and Cancun Nautical Association, created a vast and ambitious underwater sculpture park, an artistic and poignant artificial reef designed to relieve the pressures through artistic impression.

Two galleries, the 8 metre- (26 feet) deep Salon Nizuc off Cancun's shore and the 4 metre- (13 feet) deep Salon Manchones in the waters around the tiny Isla Mujeres, offer both snorkelling and scuba diving opportunities unlike anywhere else. To swim amidst the statues is both surreal and moving, their closed eyes and faces etched with expression creating a haunting and beautiful vision. Amongst the most striking of the exhibits is the 'The Silent Evolution', a collection of 450 statues based on real people which brings to life the evolution of local Mayans. From all walks of life, old and young, men and women stand together, their emotions written across their slowly eroding faces as schools of wrasse and iridescent parrotfish swim amongst them.

It took over 120 tonnes of cement, 400 kilograms (882 pounds) of silicone, 3,800 glass fibres and more than 120 hours of underwater work to install the 1,616 square metre (5,302 square feet) sculpture garden. Gliding sting rays, majestic angelfish, spiked lionfish and schools of electric blue tang dance amongst the statues, inquisitive turtles meander by, and hard and soft corals sprout from their new homes. The blending of art and the marine environment is evident throughout, but perhaps nowhere more so than at 'Man on Fire', a figure riddled with 75 holes out of which grow live cuttings of orange, venomous fire coral.

Did You Know?

The waters off Isla Mujeres are one of the best places in the world to swim alongside the planet's largest fish, the whaleshark. Measuring up to 14 metres (46 feet) in length these gentle giants arrive in their hundreds during the summer months to feed in the plankton-rich waters.

Take Me There

How to Visit: The MUSA Underwater Museum of Art can be visited from Cancun or Isla Mujeres, a small island accessed by ferry from Cancun. Most local dive centres offer guided snorkelling and scuba diving trips.

Further Information: For further information on the exhibits visit the websites of Jason deCaires Taylor **www.underwatersculpture.com** and MUSA **musacancun. org**. For more information on visiting Cancun, Isla Mujeres and Quintana Roo Mexico's Tourism website **www.visitmexico.com** is a good resource.

ANGEL FALLS
VENEZUELA

Without hesitation or even a moment to contemplate the enormity of the drop below, the river gushing across the table-top mountain of Auyántepui in the heart of remote Venezuela, plummets over the precipice. It free-falls in a magnificent train 979 metres (3,212 feet) down the sheer cliffs, before turning into a great fluffy mist as it disappears into the jungle of Devil's Canyon below. For this is the world's highest uninterrupted, year-round waterfall, a staggering 19 times higher than Niagara Falls and whose spray can be felt up to a mile away. It is a gargantuan sight, best seen in the winter months when the torrent is at its most fierce and impressive, a great steaming pour of water as though from Mother Nature's teapot.

In the north west of Venezuela is a wild and impenetrable region known as the Canaima National Park, an UNESCO designated, three-million-hectare expanse of jungle from which erupt vast, flat-topped mountains known as tepui's. The landscape is bizarre, ancient and untouched. Indigenous plants and animals have adapted to the harsh environments atop the tepuis and great rainbows swirl through the sky as hundreds of streams pour off the plateaus.

While the native Pemón name of Auyántepui – meaning Mountain of the God of Evil – plays homage to the indigenous heritage of the region, the moniker Angel Falls came about from rather different roots. The great waterfall first became known to outsiders when it was spotted by James (Jimmie) Angel, an American gold-hunting adventurer and aviator, on a solo flight above the Venezuelan jungle in 1933. Four years later he returned, in search of the legendary River of Gold, with his wife and two companions, only to crash land and get stranded atop the mountain. It took 11 days for the party to descend the tepui and a further 33 years until his little plane was lifted by helicopter from the summit. It now rests outside Ciudad Bolívar's airport.

Eight decades on and the region is as remote and wild as when Jimmie Angel first landed here. Yet as all great explorers will testify, the journey is as much the adventure as the discovery, and those embarking on a quest to the base of Angel Falls will traverse the Churun river by native wooden dugout canoe from Canaima base camp, or soar over the 2,296 square miles (700 square kilometre) table-top mountain to see the falls as they were first witnessed by Jimmie Angel.

Did You Know?

Angel Falls and the tepuis of the Canaima National Park have long inspired writers with their mystery and beauty, from Sir Arthur Conan Doyle's classic tale of dinosaur-laden lands in *The Lost World*, to the Disney/Pixar movie *Up*, whose characters go in search of Paradise Falls.

Take Me There

How to Visit: Pre-arranged trips to the falls begin with a flight to the Canaima National Park Airstrip from Caracas or Ciudad Bolivar, and then a scenic flight over the top or a boat trip up the Churun River in the rainy season.

Further Information: The Venezuela tourism website **www.think-venezuela.net** is a good source of travel information and tours can be booked through a number of operators including Latin Odyssey **www.latinodyssey.com** or Journey Latin America **www.journeylatinamerica.co.uk**.

WESTRAY TO PAPA WESTRAY
ORKNEY, SCOTLAND

There are long-haul flights, short-haul flights, and then there's the world's shortest commercial flight, a little more than a high skip between the islands of Westray and Papa Westray, part of Scotland's Orkney Isles. The tedium of air travel is rarely one of our favourite parts of the travelling experience, but when the flight lasts a grand total of 2 minutes – it can be just 47 seconds if the wind is in the right direction – it makes the entire experience a little more palatable.

When the safety demonstration takes longer than the actual flight you know there's little point closing your eyes for a nap. And you can forget the drinks trolley too. For Loganair planes take off from the tiny island of Westray to cross the sea and land 1.7 miles (2.7 kilometres) away in Papa Westray, an even smaller slip of land. Despite a ferry route making the crossing in just 25 minutes, Loganair has been hopping between the two islands every summer since 1967 and the route is a popular feature on the Orkney island-hopping circuit.

Just off the northernmost point of mainland Scotland, the Orkneys exude a rugged Celtic charm. Just 17 of the 70 islands in the archipelago are inhabited – Papa Westray managing to just be included with a population of 70 while Westray is inhabited by over 600 people – and nesting sea birds, puffins and seal colonies easily outnumber human inhabitants. The mercilessly unpredictable weather has shaped and sculpted the land, great cliffs dropping into often turbulent seas, windswept grasslands home to hardy grazing cattle and evidence of the islands' long ancestry etched across the landscape in lonely prehistoric ruins.

Westray and Papa Westray (known as Papay) are some of the remotest of the Orkney isles, just blips of land with strong, proud communities dating back thousands of years. In Westray, the ruins of the once-grand Noltland Castle are shrouded in stories of royal murder, and crumbling Viking and Neolithic remains are scattered across the cliffs and sandy beaches. Just across the channel it is hard to imagine that 4 miles- (6 kilometres) long Papay was once a centre for medieval Christian pilgrimage, the chapel of St Tredwell now just an isolated jumble of rocks. Older even than the Pyramids is the Knap of Howar, the oldest standing house in Northwest Europe, left on a sea-facing promontory wonderfully intact as though its prehistoric owners have just popped out. On maritime heaths and precipitous cliffs bird sanctuaries echo with the squawk of terns and puffins, and in the tiny towns a hard-working and hardy community thrives. While the islands might be a challenging place to live, they are nothing short of delightful to visit, and with a flight time of just two minutes you have plenty of time to explore.

Did You Know?

The world's largest whiskey collection is unsurprisingly found in Scotland. In Edinburgh's Scotch Whiskey Experience there are over 4,000 bottles on display.

Take Me There

How to Visit: There are flight and ferry connections from Aberdeen, Scrabster and Gill's Bay on the Scottish mainland, as well as routes from other Orkney islands. The flight between Westray and Papa Westray is operated by Loganair.

Further Information: Flights can be booked between the two islands online at Loganair **www.loganair.co.uk**. National **www.visitscotland.com** and regional **www. westraypapawestray.co.uk** tourism websites offer travel tips.

LAKE BAIKAL
RUSSIA

Everything about Lake Baikal is record-breaking. It has existed for 20 to 25 million years, making it the planet's oldest lake. While it's transparently clear waters allow for 40 metres (131 feet) of visibility it (quite literally) doesn't scratch the surface of a lake that delves 1,620 metres (5,315 feet) down – the deepest in the world. And although it can't take the crown for being the largest lake – that goes to the Caspian Sea – Lake Baikal has the most amount of water, holding one fifth of the earth's non-frozen fresh water, a staggering 5,500 cubic miles (23,000 cubic kilometres) – more than the United States' five Great Lakes combined.

Lake Baikal sits in the wilds of eastern Siberia, the tremendous body enveloped by soaring snow-capped mountains, thick boreal forests and over 330 cold rivers that cascade through the basin. Dozens of islands and islets are scattered across its vast surface, most uninhabited, and hot mineral springs bubble out of the thermal ground, making it easy to see why the ancient native Buryat people consider this picturesque landscape sacred.

Often dubbed the 'Galapagos of Russia' Lake Baikal is ecologically unique, two thirds of the 2,000 species of flora and fauna are endemic to the great lake. While bears, elk, lynx and other wildlife abound in the surrounding forests and mountains, the most famous residents are the Baikal seals – the world's only freshwater seals – which laze in large lumbering colonies on the rocky islands and outcrops. Within the lake's cold waters some fish species can live up to a mile under the surface, others – a favoured meal of the seals – are almost transparent.

Forming the geographical, historical and sacred heart of the lake is the largest of Baikal's islands, Olkhon, a back-to-nature destination 270 square miles (700 square kilometres) in size where birds swirl around the rocky sea cliffs and smooth rolling meadows and forests teem with deer and bears. Legends of Genghis Khan are told in folklore, shamanic traditions abound and the landscape is rich with archaeological remains.

The handful of visitors that make the journey to Lake Baikal do so with an expectation that is easily fulfilled. Trekking, wildlife-watching, kayaking and fishing take on new guises in this ecological wonderland, and in the frosty winters, when a crust of ice makes the lake traversable and the land is caked in snow, you can snowmobile, ice-cycle, dog-sled and ski.

Did You Know?

Scientists are still mystified as to how the Baikal Seals came to live in the lake, but one theory is that they arrived through a sea-passage which once linked with the Arctic Ocean. The seal's closest relatives are the Arctic ringed seals, which would support this theory.

Take Me There

How to Visit: The nearest airport is Irkutsk, with connections to Moscow. Listvyanka is a jumping off point for exploring the lake and camping is possible on Olkhorn. Alternatively it is possible to stay in Severobaikalsk in the north or Slyudyanka in the south. The Trans-Siberian Express also passes along the shores of Baikal.

Further Information: For travel information to Russia, including visas, see **www.visitrussia.org**. A good source of information on Lake Baikal is **www.lakebaikal.org** and there are many good tour companies including Baikal Explorer **www.baikalex.com** and KE Adventure **www.keadventure.com**.

LALIBELA
ETHIOPIA

It might seem an easy record to hold, considering the apparent lack of competition in the rock-hewn church world, but these monolithic buildings – carved from a single stone – can be found as far and wide as France, Turkey, Bulgaria, Armenia and Finland. Yet these churches, in their regal and widely varying forms, don't come close to the sheer size and downright impressiveness of the churches of Lalibela, Ethiopia. While Biete Medhani Alem is the largest – and takes the record-breaking prize – the collection of 11 churches together create a unique landscape, each carved from the top down through solid rock and forming a living heritage and Ethiopia's most important pilgrimage site.

Located in a rural town in the mountainous region of Ethiopia's heartland, the world heritage designated churches are a far cry from a staid museum. Each morning worshippers arrive in their traditional robes of white, red and gold, brightly-coloured umbrellas protecting them from the baking African sun, to chant and pray inside the altars. The annual pilgrimage sees Ethiopian Orthodox Christians from across the country descend on the little town, even the sick and less-able bodied winding their way up the steep mountain roads for this once-in-a-lifetime religious festival.

No-one knows for certain when the churches were hewn, although common belief is they were ordered by King Lalibela in the 12th century after he travelled to Jerusalem and returned home wanting to create his own Holy Land. For the complex does in fact resemble a mini Jerusalem, the churches split into two groups representing the earthly and heavenly Holy City – in between a trench performs its role as the Jordan River, complete with baptismal pool.

To create a building, complete with doors, windows, columns and rooms, out of one piece of solid rock is no easy feat. The churches were carved from the top down, chiselled out of monolithic blocks to create intricate and ornate buildings which not only have ceremonial passages, caves, catacombs and altars, but functional trenches and drainage ditches too. At 33.5 by 23.5 metres (110 by 77 feet) and over 11.5 metres (37 feet) high, Biete Medhani Alem is the largest, surrounded by 34 columns and containing the famous 7 kilograms (15 pounds) gold Lalibela Cross. Of all the churches however, the most remarkable is the Bet Giyorgis (St George), hewn in the shape of a cross from a perfect cube of solid rock.

This little town, with its quiet cobbled streets and distinctly Ethiopian flair, has become the country's star attraction, its churches luring not only inquisitive travellers but the hundreds of devout Christians who travel to a sacred place that has become almost as important as the Holy Land on which it was created.

Did You Know?

Ethiopia is the only country in the world to have a 13-month calendar which means it is about seven years behind countries using the Gregorian calendar.

Take Me There

How to Visit: Daily flights continue on to Lalibela from Addis Ababa's international airport. There are also two-day buses that do the journey. There are several hotels in town and guides can be hired at the churches.

Further Information: UNESCO whc.unesco.org provides extensive background on the designation of the churches. For travel information visit Travel Ethiopia **www.tourismethiopia.gov.et**.

COTAHUASI
PERU

America's Grand Canyon is known around the world, the enormous gorge carved from the red rock by the Colorado River. And while most believe it to be the world's largest canyon, it in fact doesn't even rank in the top five. For there are some truly colossal ravines out there, gouged from the planet's biggest mountain ranges. The very largest of these behemoths, Cotahuasi – and the second largest, Colca – can be found in the remote Andes of Peru. From the top, where regal condors soar, to the fierce melt-water river that courses through the bottom it measures a staggering 3,354 meters (11,004 feet) – only 163 metres (534 feet) higher than its better-known and more visited neighbour Colca, and double the depth of Grand Canyon.

Over millennia the powerful river has eroded a great chasm between snow-capped mountains in this far-flung and remote corner of Peru, a place that once formed part of the ancient Inca route leading from the coast to Cuzco, and whose mountainside terraces are strewn with remains of the great empire. Llamas and alpacas graze the terraced slopes, and tiny villages exist in the remotest of spots, their ancient Andean traditions and festivals continuing uninterrupted as they have done for centuries.

Getting to the Cotahuasi Canyon is no easy feat, a bone-shaking journey by bus from the nearest city of Arequipa taking an exhausting eight hours. Unpaved and rudimentary roads weave up and down the mountains like great dirt ribbons, past highland plateaus and precipitous walls, until finally chugging into the ancient village of Cotahuasi. For those who aren't seasoned kayakers willing to tackle the relentless class IV and V rapids of the river, the village is the gateway to the canyon. Hiking trails lead steeply up to lakes and wind-moulded rock forests, past waterfalls and cactus fields, or down towards the river where ancient stone paths cling to the side of the gorge alongside the thundering river.

Waterfalls tumble down the steep walls, the grandest of them all being Sipia, a 153 metre- (502 feet) high torrent of ice-cold melt water. As if by some divine reward for the ardours of getting to this faraway spot, hot springs emerge from the ground to soothe and rejuvenate tired feet, and fruit trees grow stubbornly in the oasis that snakes its way between the arid mountains. Whether under your own steam or as part of a handful of tours that guide intrepid travellers here, you'll find Cotahuasi an authentic and wild destination, a place governed by the whims of the canyon.

Did You Know?

Ranking canyons in size is a tricky job and geologists have debated it for years. Other contenders for the deepest canyon are the Yarlung Tsangpo Grand Canyon in Tibet, the Indus Gorge in the Himalayas and the Kali Gandaki Gorge in Nepal.

Take Me There

How to Visit: Public buses run to Cotahuasi from the city of Arequipa (8–10 hours) or alternatively 4-wheel-drive vehicles can be rented (note: the road from Chuquibamba is not paved and very steep). There are many rustic hostels in Cotahuasi.

Further Information: To start planning a trip to Peru visit the tourism authority website **www.visitperu.com**. There are several outfits offering tours including Peru Adventure Tours **www.peruadventuretours.com** and Turismo Inkaiko **www.turismoinkaiko.com**.

IRONBRIDGE
SHROPSHIRE, ENGLAND

The year was 1709 and in a workshop in the small village of Coalbrookdale, on the shores of the River Severn gorge, a man by the name of Abraham Darby was busy working away trying to prove that it was possible to smelt iron ore with coke made from local coal. It was, and he did. What he couldn't have known however, was that his discovery, and the iron bridge his grandson would build 70 years later, would change the face of the world and rocket this little Shropshire village into the history books as the birthplace of the Industrial Revolution.

Darby's discovery saw Coalbrookdale begin mass-producing the first iron wheels, engines and rails at a rate not seen elsewhere before. But it wasn't until 1779 when his grandson, Abraham Darby III built a 30 metre (100 feet) cast iron bridge across the River Severn that the eye of the world turned on Coalbrookdale – which was quickly re-named Ironbridge when engineers, iron magnates and Victorian and Edwardian tourists descended on it to gawp at a bridge not made in stone or wood but of 378 tonnes of iron. The bridge opened on New Year's Day 1781, a day that can be seen as a major turning point in the Industrial Revolution. It is Britain's best-known industrial monument and remains to this day the *pièce de résistance* of the Ironbridge Gorge – even the Queen has walked across it.

Today in the sleepy, quaint village of Ironbridge, where cottages tumble down the wooded slopes of the gorge, the once smoke-belching furnaces, factories and ship-laden canals have been replaced by museums, and tourists still come to see for themselves the 30 metre (100 feet) wide bridge. The original buildings remain, and in them ten different museums tell the story of a Quaker family, their iron-smelting village and the revolution that ensued. The Victorian mansion houses of the Darby family can be visited, with their grand river-facing façades, original furniture and quaint dress-up rooms. Inside the aptly named Tar Tunnel, bitumen seeps through the walls from a sticky black spring struck over 200 years ago – hard hat in place you can walk the dim, brick-lined passageway. Visit the factories of once famous British merchants which have changed little since they closed in the 1950's; the colourful ceramics of the Jackfield Tile Factory, the world-exported clay tobacco pipes of the Broseley Pipeworks, and the fine china of the Coalport China Factory. There is even a Victorian town, complete with smells, sounds and costumed locals. And of course in the midst of it all is the bridge, a beautiful Grade I listed, UNESCO designated arch of iron which sits serenely above the still waters, as possibly the most important bridge ever built.

Did You Know?

The modern Olympic Games have their roots in the tiny village of Much Wenlock in Shropshire. Dr William Penny Brookes, a lifelong resident, started a village games and later became one of the founding fathers of the modern-day sporting event.

Take Me There

How to Visit: There is an international airport in Birmingham which serves the town of Telford from which public transport connects to Ironbridge and the surrounding museums.

Further Information: The Ironbridge websites **www.ironbridge.org.uk; www.visitironbridge.co.uk** provide practical tips on visiting the bridge and museums while the Shropshire Tourism website **www.shropshiretourism.co.uk** has a thorough guide to the county.

THE EMPTY QUARTER
(RUB' AL KHALI), ARABIA

It is a simple description and a name so perfect that there leaves no doubt as to its essence. The Empty Quarter (Rub' al Khali in Arabic) is a vast swathe of fine, fiery orange sand that blankets the southern part of the Arabian Peninsula, forming the largest sand desert on the planet. It is an area the size of France or Texas – 250,000 square miles (650,000 square kilometres) – with absolutely nothing in it.

Since long before records began, nomadic Bedouin tribes and their camel caravans have traversed the great sand sea, whose blurred borders occupy Saudi Arabia, Oman, the United Arab Emirates and Yemen. It is a place where the dunes tower 250 metres (820 feet) into the air, great salmon-coloured mountains that shift with the winds, and where temperatures can go from a skin blistering 56°C (133°F) to below freezing when the hot sun has set in a hue of orange and pink.

Against all odds life does survive in this barren and inhospitable world where nothing but sand stretches to the horizon and the silence rings in your ears. Scorpions, gazelles, Arabian Oryx and a few hardy plants have adapted to the hyper-arid conditions. Proud Bedouins tend their camels, goats and sheep, each the other's lifeline in this unforgiving world where time seemingly stands still – or perhaps isn't even measured. Until AD300, when the sand became unpassable, trade caravans sailed across the region, bringing with them frankincense from Arabia. Today, the modern day treasure of oil has been discovered beneath the dunes, and oil fields sit in the remotest of corners of the Empty Quarter – Al-Ghawar being the largest in the world.

When the great explorer Wilfred Thesiger embarked across the Empty Quarter in the 1940s he did so under the intuitive guidance of the Bedouin. His footsteps might have long been swept away by the hot winds, but his legacy has lasted, and the romance and sheer empty beauty attracts those in search of tranquillity and deafening silence. Oman and the United Arab Emirates are the most popular jumping off points into the desert, a handful of luxury hotels dotting the fringes from where 4-wheel-drive and camel trips embark. Multi-day trips get you out into the feral heart of the region, where you sleep under the blackest of skies and brightest of stars, watch the flamingo-pink sun set behind the sand hills, or go in search of the Bedouins as they roam through the vastness of what is one of Earth's most merciless yet starkly beautiful landscapes.

Take Me There

How to Visit: The Empty Quarter is most commonly visited from UAE through Liwa Oasis (a 124 mile/200 kilometre drive from Abu Dhabi) and from Oman. It is also possible from Saudi Arabia. There are several good hotels, and multi-day tours can be arranged in advance.

Further Information: There are many tour operators offering excursions into the desert including Original Travel **www.originaltravel.co.uk**, Oman Trekking Guides **www. omantrekkingguides.com** and Abercrombie and Kent **www. abercrombiekent.co.uk**. The Oman **www.omantourism.gov. com** and Abu Dhabi **visitabudhabi.ae** tourism websites provide helpful travel planning guides.

Did You Know?

Desert oases are a lifeline for people and animals in the otherwise bleak and arid deserts. The world's largest oasis is the Nile Valley covering approximately 8,500 square miles (22,000 square kilometres).

SAN PEDRO SULA
HONDURAS

It's not a title any city wants for itself, but the grim reality is that Honduras' second largest city is a dangerous place to live. Gang wars are rife and it has a murder rate of 173 per 100,000 people – the highest of any city outside of a war zone. An average 3.3 people are murdered in San Pedro Sula every day, and 83% of these homicides are from illegal firearms.

Another undeniable fact is that Honduras is a beautiful, culturally-rich country. Located in the heart of Central America, it stretches from the Pacific to the Caribbean, its interior a mixture of national parks, Mayan relics and colonial towns. The Bay Islands attract scuba divers and sun-worshipper's who come to swim with dolphins and whale sharks and relax in the idyllic tropical surroundings. Along the coast, sweeping beaches are home to towns steeped in pirate history and traditional Garifuna villages. The Pico Bonito Mountain towers above the national park of the same name, whose mangroves are home to manatees, anteaters and rainbow-coloured birds. Heading inland, through rolling green hills blanketed in banana, coffee and tobacco plantations evidence of Mayan ancestry is everywhere. The great archaeological remains at Copán are amongst the most significant in Central America, and the picturesque town is characterised by cobbled stone streets and bohemian artists' shops.

But to get to any of these places involves venturing through San Pedro Sula, the main transport hub in the east of the country. While on the surface, especially during daylight hours, the violence is not immediately evident, a closer look reveals heavily fortified buildings, soldiers patrolling the streets and a population living in fear of gang retribution. As a main thoroughfare for the illegal transport of drugs between South and North America, Honduras' drug gangs rule the roost, and barrios (ghettoes) honour only the laws of the street. Even in San Pedro Sula's lawless prisons, gang leaders control who enters, and who leaves in a body bag.

Honduras is a passionate country, where religion, tradition and family are the cornerstones of society and where love for the national football team is legendary. Yet it is also a country suffering from political upheavals and rampant gang wars. Despite the grisly and unsavoury distinction of being the world's most dangerous city, San Pedro Sula offers visitors a gateway to the untamed tropical adventures on its doorstep.

Did You Know?

The 21st December 2012 was regarded as the last date on the 5,126-year-long Mayan calendar and many believed it foretold the end of the world. Of course the prophecies didn't come true and so certain were they of the outcome NASA published a video titled 'Why the World Didn't End Yesterday' on the 20th December.

Take Me There

How to Visit: San Pedro Sula's international airport is the main transport hub for the east of Honduras and receives flights from the United States, Mexico and Central American countries. There are chain hotels in the city centre and several good guesthouses. Public bus transport to other parts of the country is efficient and safe.

Further Information: For advice and tips on planning a trip to Honduras the tourism authority website www.letsgohonduras.com is a good first resource.

THE GREAT BLUE HOLE
BELIZE

At first glance Belize's Great Blue Hole appears to be a trick on the eye, a dark abyss that seemingly disappears into the denizens of the deep. But as the famed local saying goes; 'You'd better Belize-it'. For the world's largest blue hole is in fact just that. As though a giant plug has been plucked from the pale turquoise waters of Lighthouse Reef atoll, the hole is perfectly round, measuring 300 metres (984 feet) in diameter and dropping to an eerie 124 metres (406 feet) deep.

When Jacques Cousteau sailed his ship *Calypso* here in 1971 he declared it one of the world's top ten dive sites, a declaration that has found the Blue Hole on scuba diving and snorkelling bucket lists to this day. Ringed by corals, which at low tide poke above the surface of the warm water, the great chasm sits at the heart of the atoll 43 miles (70 kilometres) from the mainland.

Plunging under the surface of the submarine sinkhole reveals an otherworldly and ancient landscape. Caves and passageways pocket the walls, massive limestone stalactites dangle from overhangs like Stone Age chandeliers, and stalagmites that formed in the once air-filled caverns date back to the last Ice Age and a time when sea levels were much lower. Millions of years ago the ceiling collapsed and, as the oceans rose, the water poured in, filling the cathedral-like caverns and plunging the floor into darkness once again.

Today Caribbean reef sharks circle slowly, their unmistakable shapes silhouetted against the blue sky. The odd curious black tip, tiger or hammerhead shark makes an appearance, delicate angelfish and butterfly fish dart in and out of the hollows and elk horn coral and purple sea fans sway in the shallows.

Far from the lively, bohemian atmosphere of Caye Caulker and Ambergris Caye, the outer lying atolls are remote and isolated. The Maya once inhabited these tiny coral islands, although the English names of Glover's and Turneffe reefs pay homage to the pirates who plied these waters. Visitors to Lighthouse Reef arrive in search of subaquatic wonders, where diving and snorkelling reveals stingrays and barracudas, schools of yellow snappers, octopus and turtles which inhabit the sea grass meadows of Half Moon Caye National Monument. It is one of Belize's largest protected areas and home to a 4,000-member colony of blue-footed booby birds, one of the largest in the world outside of the Galapagos Islands.

Did You Know?

In 1975 Jacques Cousteau discovered the wreck of the HMHS *Brittanic*, the largest ship lost in the First World War. As the sister ship to the RMS *Titanic*, *Brittanic* was built as an ocean cruise liner but was commissioned to serve as a hospital war ship before being sunk by a mine off the Greek Island of Kea in 1916.

Take Me There

How to Visit: Trips to Lighthouse Reef and the Blue Hole can be arranged from Caye Caulker and Ambergris Caye. There are numerous dive centres offering trips, and scenic flights can also be arranged.

Further Information: The tourism website www.travelbelize.org offers practical information on visiting Belize. There is a variety of accommodation on Caye Caulker and Ambergris Caye, from bohemian lodges to wooden huts. Accommodation on the outer reefs includes Itza Lodge www.itzalodge.com and Turneffe Resort www.turnefferesort.com.

THE PALACE OF PARLIAMENT
BUCHAREST, ROMANIA

Few people describe the façade of Bucharest's Palace of Parliament as beautiful, its stout neo-classical architecture more grand and formidable than elegant and graceful. Yet it is undoubtedly impressive – and simply enormous. While the building stands robustly as the heaviest in the world, it is also the second largest administrative building after the Pentagon, and the most expensive ever built – an estimated US$4 billion.

There are few buildings in history which have evoked such fervent emotions as the Palace of Parliament. The once Communist behemoth was initially reviled by the city's residents, its construction seen as rubbing salt in the wounds of a country suffering from poverty and the aftermath of a devastating earthquake. When it was commissioned in 1984 by the Communist leader Nicolae Ceausescu, it was to be his megalomaniacal crowning glory, the ambitious and grandiose headquarters of his government. Great swathes of the city centre were demolished to make way for a building so large it is visible from space, and 9,000 homes, churches and synagogues were razed almost overnight.

Ceausescu hadn't quite finished his extravagant and costly project when the Romanian Revolution saw an end to communism, but the question of what to do with the conspicuous reminder of such a dark era remained. Today Ceausescu's controversial 'People's Palace' houses the country's parliament and Romanians are beginning to make their peace with its presence. It acts as an international conference centre – it hosted the 2008 NATO summit – and a place where weddings are celebrated and balls hosted. Celebrities and politicians from Michael Jackson to Vladimir Putin and Shakira to George Bush have been guests.

Constructing one of the largest and most lavish buildings on the planet is no easy feat and the statistics are mind-boggling; it took 20,000 workers and 700 architects to build the 12 stories, 1,100 rooms, (at least) eight subterranean floors and a vast nuclear bunker. It is 270 metres (885 feet) long, 240 metres (787 feet) wide and measures 350,000 square meters (3.77 million square feet) – the equivalent of 280 Olympic size swimming pools. One crystal chandelier alone weighs 2.5 tonnes (5,000 pounds). And it would take an hour just to walk the perimeter.

Guided tours reveal halls the size of football pitches luxuriously adorned with oak panelling, floors swathed in plush carpets up to 600 square metres (1,968 square feet) in size and beautiful stained glass windows. Visitors are left slack-jawed by the mountain of a building which is said to have been built from two mountains of marble. Combined with the 700,000 tonnes (1.5 billion pounds) of steel and bronze and 3,500 tonnes (7.7 million pounds) of crystal glass it is the heaviest building in the world, and one which weighed even heavier on the people of Romania.

Take Me There

How to Visit: The Palace of Parliament is in the centre of Bucharest and can be reached by air through the city's international airport. Tours of the building last two hours.

Further Information: Advice and information on visiting Romania is provided by the official tourism website **romaniatourism.com**. For further information on tours, visit **www.cdep.ro**.

Did You Know?

Rumour has it that the Palace of Parliament was designed on North Korean architecture after Ceausescu sent architects to visit to Pyongyang's Grand People's Study House.

CRATER LAKE
TAAL VOLCANO, PHILIPPINES

Like a set of beautiful Russian dolls, the lakes and islands of Taal Volcano unravel in size, each nesting amidst the other in one of the world's most unique geological phenomena. It is mind-boggling to imagine a lake on an island in a lake on an island, but that is precisely what Crater Lake is – the top of the volcanic pyramid. Crater Lake is on Volcano Island in Taal Lake on the main island of Luzon in the Philippines, and is the largest, but by no means only, one of these concentric features.

Taal Volcano is one of the world's top 20 deadliest prehistoric volcanoes, once towering 5,500 metres (18,000 feet) into the air, and which has taken thousands of lives in its devastating past. It has rocked the region with 33 eruptions, and while the last was in 1977, it has been rumbling ominously since 1991, making it the second most active volcano along the Philippines' 'Ring of Fire'. All the eruptions come from Volcano Island in the centre of Taal Lake, the island peak, in fact the tip of Taal Volcano which simmers beneath the waters. Just a few hundred years ago Taal Lake was a part of the ocean – an arm of the Balayan Bay – that was cut off after a series of violent eruptions filled the entrance to the channel. Over the past three centuries, the seawater gradually turned brackish and then fresh, the ocean-dwelling inhabitants evolving to their new environment. Today, rare freshwater sardines swim in the 15 miles (24 kilometre)-wide lake, and a freshwater snake – one of only two in the world – thrives here. Bull sharks once inhabited the waters but these were hunted to extinction by local fishermen in the 1930s.

Standing on the dramatic 600 metre- (2,000 feet) high Tagatay Ridge – once a part of the original super volcano – Taal Lake, Volcano Island and Crater Lake make a stunning vista. Shimmering alluringly below, the lakes draw visitors to explore the very heart of a volcano that once devastated the villages that inhabited its slopes, but which today is one of the country's most picturesque national parks. Small traditional boats trundle across the lake from the charming village of Talisay to Volcano Island from where hikes lead to the shores of Crater Lake. Like a black gemstone sitting in the very summit of the volcano its waters are highly sulphuric and no life exists.

Did You Know?

For many years it was believed that Vulcan Point inside Crater Lake was the largest island in a lake on an island in a lake on an island. It has since been discovered that an uninhabited series of lakes and islands in Lake Manitou, Canada is the largest of this unusual phenomenon.

Take Me There

How to Visit: Talisay is the gateway to the region and can be reached easily from Manila. Day trips from the capital are possible with a variety of tours. There are volcano tours, watersports facilities and accommodation options in the village.

Further Information: The regional **www.talisaybatangas. gov.ph** and national **www.itsmorefuninthephillippines.com** tourism authorities offer good resources to help plan a trip to Taal Lake.

HIGHWAY 1
AUSTRALIA

Imagine driving from London to Ulanbataar, Mongolia's capital city in the far eastern stretches of the bleak Gobi Desert... and back again. That's the same distance as circumnavigating Australia's Highway 1, a vast ring road that wraps around the island continent. A network of highways join to form the enormous road, which is a staggering 9,000 miles (14,500 kilometres) long, a mishmash of multi-lane freeways which sweep around the big cities to two-lane roads in deep rural areas, and the odd single-lane in the truly remote outback.

Every day more than a million people travel on some part of the highway. In other parts there are great stretches where kangaroos are more frequently seen than vehicles. There are more direct routes around Australia's enormous terrain, yet none are as scenic and spectacular as Highway 1, the road curving past bustling coastal cities, dramatic coastlines, remote deserts, tropical rainforests and iconic sights.

The spectacular Great Ocean Road between Melbourne and Adelaide flies along the southern coast past wild surfing beaches and the iconic Twelve Apostles rocks. It blends seamlessly into the poker-straight Eyre Highway which crosses the pancake-flat Nullarbor Plain desert on its long and remote way to Western Australia.

The Pacific Highway whizzes north from the effervescent Sydney, and up into Queensland's Gold Coast with views across the Great Barrier Reef, the picturesque Fraser Island and the vibrant Sunshine Coast. From wild and far-flung Western Australia – where Highway 1 hugs the coast past Perth and the Ningaloo Reef teeming with marine life – to the northern reaches where it passes through thick forests and great coastal national parks, it traverses every Aussie state. It even dips offshore to Tasmania, circling the Cradle Mountain-Lake, St Clair National Park with its jagged peaks and glacial lakes.

It is impossible to get lost on Highway 1, the long stretches of tarmac disappearing seemingly endlessly into the heat hazed horizon. Driving the entire route is an epic adventure that can take you from 34°C in the north to sub-zero in the south, from the tree-climbing kangaroos of Kakadu National Park to the whalesharks of Exmouth. Hiring a campervan or motorhome allows great freedom, but there are hundreds of hotels, hostels and campsites along the route too. Embarking on the entire journey is not one for the faint-hearted, but to experience all of Australia, without ever coming off the highway, is the ultimate road trip.

Did You Know?

Australia's Dingo Fence, which stretches from the Queensland coast 3,488 miles (5,614 kilometres) across the country to the Nullabor Plain, was built in the 1880s to protect the fertile southern lands from dingoes. It is more than twice the length of the Great Wall of China and the world's longest unbroken fence.

Take Me There

How to Visit: If you visit Australia you will at some point find yourself on Highway 1. To embark on a longer road trip it is possible to hire cars, campervans or motorhomes from all the big cities.

Further Information: Australia's national **www.australia.com** and regional **www.visitgreatoceanroad.org.au**; **www.visit-queensland.com** websites provide comprehensive guides to the country and are good starting points for planning a trip.

MOYENNE ISLAND
SEYCHELLES

When Brendon Grimshaw first stepped foot on Moyenne Island in 1962, it was love at first sight. The British journalist, searching for a new home and new way of life in the Indian Ocean paradise of the Seychelles, saw in the tiny scrap of overgrown land, ignored and rejected by even the region's wildlife, an undeniable beauty. He paid just £8,000 (US$13,000) for his tropical home, and so began six decades of a labour of love during which time he was offered – and rejected – up to $50 million for his home.

This real-life Robison Crusoe began the arduous task of clearing the tangle of jungle that spread to the sandy shores of his little island, helped along the way by long-time friend Rene Antoine Lafortune, a local Seychellois. Over the decades, a delightful maze of footpaths appeared, steps were hewn out of the rocks, 16,000 trees were planted and 120 rare Seychelles giant tortoises were brought to live alongside Grimshaw, Moyenne's one and only human resident. The slow and regal tortoises, indigenous to the Seychelles but under threat on many of the developed islands, were soon joined by flocks of birds and the island became a flourishing nature reserve.

Sitting amidst idyllic turquoise waters and protected by a ring of coral reef, Moyenne is the quintessential storybook tropical island, where tales of pirate treasure have been passed down through legend. While some believe the lost treasure of the infamous pirate Olivier Levasseur might be hidden somewhere on Moyenne, to this day it remains hidden, perhaps guarded by the two unidentified graves discovered there.

Once a part of the St Anne Marine Park, Moyenne was designated an independent national park following Grimshaw's death in 2012 – a fitting testament to his years of dedication. Its neighbouring islands are an eclectic mix of private luxury retreats, rustic, laid-back Gardens of Eden or princely playgrounds, and all steeped in the often turbulent history of the region. Seagrass meadows are home to turtles and an abundance of fish, and dolphins visit the protected waters.

Even though the enigmatic Grimshaw is no longer there to delight visitors with his tales of pirate ghosts, sharks and tropical storms, Moyenne's unique character and colourful history are undeniable. Rustling palm trees sway in the breeze, the rustic 'Jolly Roger' restaurant serves local dishes and the island's last residents, Grimshaw's giant tortoises, plod happily through their lives on their very own island paradise.

Did You Know?

Giant tortoises are the oldest living animals on the planet. Indeed, it is believed that the current oldest living creature is a Seychelles Giant Tortoise named Jonathan, who is 182 years old and lives a celebrity existence in the grounds of the governor's house on the island of St Helena.

Take Me There

How to Visit: Moyenne Island can be easily visited for the day from the capital of Victoria on Seychelles' main island of Mahe. A trip to the island can be incorporated into a visit around the St Anne Marine Park, and there are numerous boat tour companies offering excursions.

Further Information: The Seychelles National Parks Authority **www.snpa.sc** provides information on opening hours, park entry fees and the history and ecology of the region.

ABU SIMBEL
EGYPT

For 3,200 years the colossal temple of Abu Simbel stood on the shores of the River Nile amidst a landscape scattered with remains from ancient Egypt. Carved into the limestone mountain was the grandest temple of them all built by the mighty pharaoh Ramses II, whose reign lasted 67 years. In the 1960s the creation of the Aswan High Dam and resulting Lake Nasser threatened to submerge Abu Simbel beneath the rising waters. And so it was moved. All staggering (estimated) 35,000 tonnes (77,161,792 pounds) of it.

Ancient Egyptian engineers were masters at their craft, and Ramses' elaborate temple (in fact there were two temples joined together) was not only enormous and intricately adorned, but held an impressive architectural secret. On the main temple four 20 metre- (65 feet) tall statues of Ramses sat guarding its 35 metre- (115 feet) wide façade which is topped by a frieze of 22 baboons. Hidden behind the entrance a series of grand halls and chambers lead to the inner sanctuary deep in the heart of the mountain. It is here, where the deified Ramses II sits alongside three of the most powerful Egyptian gods, where Abu Simbel's true magic happens. For on October 21st and January 21st every year the sun aligns with the entrance shining a beam of light along the halls to illuminate three of the gods. The fourth, the god of the underworld, remains in darkness.

It was this most special feature that was the biggest challenge for 2,000 engineers and archaeologists who responded to Egypt's plea for help to the UN. With time ticking and the waters of Lake Nasser rising the decision was made to move the colossal monument out of harm's way. Contractors from 51 countries worked together to carve Abu Simbel into over 1,000 blocks, each weighing up to 30 tonnes, and move it to a higher elevation 213 metres (700 feet) away. It was one of the most ambitious structural moves in history, a vast game of lego played with some of the world's most precious relics.

Today Abu Simbel stands in its new home, where the sun still finds Ramses twice a year and bathes him in light. Both the temples – the second, smaller one built for Ramses' queen Nefertari – are one of Egypt's top destinations, where visitors arrive from nearby Aswan or swoop in for a fleeting visit by plane to the nearby airstrip. The magnitude of the temple is breathtaking, where the great statues of Ramses loom over all who visit just as he planned all those years ago. What he couldn't have planned however, was the passionate modern-day rescue that ensued to save his beloved temple.

Did You Know?

Abu Simbel might be the heaviest building ever moved but the heaviest building to be relocated *intact* is the Fu Gang building in Guangxi Province, China. The multi-story building weighs 15,140 tonnes, and in 2004 took 11 days to move 36 metres (118 feet).

Take Me There

How to Visit: Both temples are open to visitors and tour buses depart from Aswan, the nearest city 176 miles (282 kilometres) away. There is also an airfield nearby which receives regular tourist flights.

Further Information: The Egypt tourism authority **www.egypt.travel** offers useful advice on visiting the monument, and background information is provided by UNESCO **whc.unesco.org**.

MOSQUITO BAY
VIEQUES ISLAND, PUERTO RICO

It is difficult to imagine bombs splashing into the sparkling Caribbean waters of Vieques Island, throwing great clouds of perfect white sand into the air. Yet from 1946 until 2003 this idyllic, tropical little island just 8 miles (13 kilometres) off the coast of Puerto Rico was almost wholly inhabited by the US Army who used it for training, testing and exercise. A lot has changed for Vieques in the last decade. The military zone is now a flourishing National Wildlife Refuge, the island is home to some of the Caribbean's most picturesque, palm-fringed beaches and it has been officially recognised as having the world's brightest bioluminescence.

Vieques remains a wonderfully off-the-beaten-path destination, a refreshingly undeveloped Caribbean island where wild horses roam the interior forests, iguanas bathe in the sunshine and a handful of accommodation options range from rustic beach huts to unpretentious boutique spas. Amidst the tangle of dense coastal mangroves is a rare and fragile ecosystem, where the perfect combination of circumstances has created the ideal home for billions of tiny microscopic organisms known as dinoflagellates.

When agitated these miniscule plankton emit a flash of neon turquoise light, together creating a magical glow in the deep waters of Mosquito Bay lagoon. While bioluminescence can be found in seas across the world, the unique environment of Vieques – which is home to several of these lagoons – has resulted in over 160,000 'dinos' per litre of water. Fed by the mangrove trees and penned in to the cool, deep waters of the lagoon by a narrow channel, the plankton thrives in the undeveloped environment of the bay, where even fish create a trail of light like shooting stars through the water.

After the sun has set, and preferably on the very darkest nights, you can set off on an otherworldly kayaking adventure through the mangrove channels and into the sparkling waters of the lagoon. Like an aquatic northern lights a glowing green wake swirls behind the canoe, and each dip of the oar produces glittering drops like emeralds splashing onto the surface. Electric boats also offer tours of the bay, their eco-friendly motors protecting the delicate environment, in what is surely one of the most romantic and ethereal places on the planet.

Did You Know?

Until recently, sliding into the dark waters of Mosquito Bay and watching as bodies were enveloped in an alien-like glow was allowed and even encouraged. However conservationists believe that this sensitive ecosystem can be irreparably damaged by chemicals such as insect repellents and lotions and it is now against the law to swim in the bay. Be sure to book with a licensed and responsible tour operator and help preserve the beauty and unique ecological value of Vieques Island.

Take Me There

How to Visit: Passenger ferries make the 1 hour 15 minute journey between Fajardo on Puerto Rico's main island and Vieques several times a day, and there are various flight options including the 30 minute trip from San Juan International Airport with Cape Air www.capeair.com.

Further Information: Puerto Rico's tourism website www.seepuertorico.com offers a list of reputable tour companies running kayaking or boating trips in Mosquito Bay.

THE EDEN PROJECT
CORNWALL, ENGLAND

Wandering through the mist-shrouded rainforest, the earthy scents and chatter of birds mix with the distant trickle of a waterfall. Vines cling to the trees, great bunches of ripe bananas hang from the highest branches and tall bamboo grasses sway gently. While it may certainly look and feel like the depths of South America's rainforest, this flourishing ecosystem is actually on the other side of the world in a sleepy corner of Cornwall, England – in a very big greenhouse.

The world's largest greenhouses – there are in fact two – resemble huge bubbles erupting from the ground within which thousands of exotic species have been nurtured into verdant mini ecosystems. They were built as part of the Eden Project, an ambitious attraction and education facility which filled the hole of a mine that was, in its heyday, the centre of life in the quiet village of St Blazey. Today, plants, flowers and trees from every corner of the globe fill the two biomes, paths weaving between ponds, streams and statues.

Formed of hundreds of hexagonal, inflated, plastic cells the biomes are meticulously regulated to optimum temperature and moisture. Measuring a staggering 55 metres (180 feet) high, 100 metres (328 feet) wide and 200 metres (656 feet) long, the tropical biome is the biggest of the two and houses the world's largest captive rainforest. Rubber and nut trees jostle for space between spices, coffee and cocoa plants, a high walkway weaves amongst the canopy, and Malaysian huts and African totem sculptures add a dash of culture. Entering the Mediterranean biome next door, the hot humidity is left behind as the heady aromas of lemons and perfumed herbs evoke a sense of balmy coastal Spain. Giant aloe vera plants spread their thick leaves, citrus trees hang heavy with plump fruit and vines drip with bunches of grapes. There are gnarled olive and cork trees, bright springtime tulips and colourful flowers from as far afield as California and South Africa. Outside of the greenhouses temperate plants grow under the Cornish sky, as paths weave between sweet lavender, tea, hops, hemp and bright sunflowers.

Environmental awareness is the backbone of the Eden Project and is evident everywhere, from the energy powered by local wind turbines to the rainwater irrigation systems and the local, fair trade food in the cafes. There is even a giant statue made entirely from waste and an admission discount if you show up without a car. The Biblical Garden of Eden was filled with all the world's edible, medicinal and most beautiful plants, and here in Cornwall the Eden Project is doing a pretty good job of living up to its name.

Did You Know?

Every July the Eden Project hosts a music concert. In past years it has welcomed artists such as Amy Winehouse, James Morrison, Muse, Pulp, The Verve and Kaiser Chiefs.

Take Me There

How to Visit: The Eden Project is just outside St Blazey near the town of St Austell from which there are public transport links. The region offers plenty of tourist facilities and accommodation including B&B's, hotels and self-catering cottages.

Further Information: The Eden Project website **www. edenproject.com** contains a wealth of information on ecology, visiting and upcoming events. The Cornwall Tourism Office **www. visitcornwall.com** offers a comprehensive trip planning guide.

MOUNT CHIMBORAZO
ECUADOR

Until the 1852 discovery of the Himalayas' mighty Mount Everest, it was believed that Ecuador's Mount Chimborazo was the highest mountain in the world. But while the crown slipped off the summit of Chimborazo, it was a short-lived disappointment. For Mount Everest is in fact the tallest mountain on earth, not the highest – and there is a very big difference. Measured from sea level Chimborazo falls 2,580 metres (8464 feet) short of the Himalayan giant, but because of the shape of Earth– which bulges like an oval at the equator – Mount Chimborazo's summit is about 1.3 miles (2.1 kilometres) farther from the centre of the earth than Everest's. And so Ecuador's highest peak once again wears its crown proudly as the highest point in the world, the furthest from the centre of the earth and the closest point on the planet to outer space.

The mountain is huge, standing at 6,310 metres (20,720 feet.) tall and 78 miles (125 kilometres) in circumference. Its four dormant peaks are riddled with glaciers and year-round snow covers its upper slopes. In the crisp blue air of the Andes its conical peak can be seen for over a hundred miles along the Ecuadorian coast towering above its neighbours in a region known as the Avenida de los Volcanes (Avenue of Volcanoes). Its lower slopes are protected by the Reserva de Produccion Faunistica Chimborazo, a national park created to preserve the habitat of the herds of woolly llamas, alpacas and vicuña that thrive in the chilly, thin air.

The world's extreme places have long lured the great explorers, who ventured into unknown dangers simply to discover the unknown, and Chimborazo was the ultimate challenge. In 1746 the French scientists who are attributed with proving the world isn't perfectly round failed to reach the summit. So too did the famed explorer Alexander von Humboldt. It wasn't until 1886 that English climber Edward Whymper and his two Italian guides finally reached the world's highest point.

Climbing Mount Chimborazo is a serious undertaking and hikers must be accompanied by a guide. Setting out from the nearby town of Riobamba in the dark early hours, you make your way up the volcano along the Whymper Route arriving mid-morning at the summit. While a round-trip takes around 10 hours, the going is tough and proper equipment imperative. Two refuges on the lower slopes are a wonderful alternative for the less experienced who want to explore the landscape, see the llamas and vicuñas, and get a closer look at the very tip of the world.

Did You Know?

On 15 August 1976, a flight en route from Quito to Cuenca carrying 59 people went missing in the Ecuadorian Andes. It wasn't until 27 years later that climbers looking for a new route to the summit of Mount Chimborazo found the plane and all passengers 200 metres (656 feet) from the top.

Take Me There

How to Visit: The nearest town is Riobamba which can be reached by public transport from Quito. It is possible to explore the lower slopes of the mountain independently but all climbers must be accompanied by an accredited mountain guide of which there are many in the town.

Further Information: The Ecuador tourism website **ecuador.travel/en** is a good resource for planning a trip.

ICEHOTEL
JUKKASJÄRVI, SWEDEN

Far above the Arctic Circle, the frosty landscape of Sweden's Lapland is another world. The Northern Lights swirl in dark winter skies in a sultry dance of green, purple and red. The snow-blanketed ground shimmers like a million diamonds have been scattered haphazardly across it, and the raging Torne River stands silently still. In this frozen wonderland, the world's largest ice hotel – memorably named ICEHOTEL – not so much resides within it but is crafted from it.

A night spent in the 5,500 square metre (8,000 square feet) ICEHOTEL requires a wilderness-style orientation and a very thick sleeping bag – both of which are highly appreciated as the rooms are a chilly -5°C. Built from great slabs of ice carved out of the River Torne in March, the 65 rooms are rebuilt each year, only to melt away a few months later when the sun returns to this northern stretch. It is a year-round cycle, a project built from passion and artistic expression that is at the mercy of the extreme seasons. Spring sees the harvesting of the 2,500, man-sized blocks of pure ice – stored in chilled warehouses – and early winter brings with it a flurry of artists and engineers who come to carve life into the sculpted ice rooms. The frozen doors open in December where, for four months, 50,000 people descend on the village of Jukkasjärvi, to experience this artistic exhibition and engineering masterpiece.

Without plumbing and bathroom facilities – and because the bed is made from a giant chunk of ice – most stay just one night in the cold rooms. Next door the 'warm' hotel is full-service, with saunas, restaurants and roaring fires. Artists from around the globe apply to design the ice suites, each room and each year bringing with it a smörgåsbord of styles and visions – from snowballs to dragons.

The hotel started life as a modest igloo built to showcase local Sami crafts. Thirty years later it is the world's biggest igloo, thirty thousand tonnes of snow and four thousand tonnes of ice creating a world-famous hotel – even the Smirnoff Vodka-sponsored ICE BARs can be found as far away as London, built from Torne River ice, and there is a chapel where couples can marry under turquoise ice arches.

Jukkasjärvi is a tiny village in remote Lapland, one of Europe's last wildernesses and a place where summer brings 100 days of midnight sun and indigenous Sami people herd reindeer through forests blanketed in winter snowfall. While summer is the time for fishing in the river, white water rafting and cross-country cycling, winter brings snowmobile and dog sled excursions, northern lights viewing, wildlife spotting and ice sculpting.

Did You Know?

The Northern Lights – or Aurora Borealis – are frequently viewed in the arctic realms of Canada, Scandinavia, Alaska, Norway and Greenland. However, on very rare occasions, when particle conditions are just right, they have been seen as far south as Kentucky, California and southern England.

Take Me There

How to Visit: The ICEHOTEL and village of Jukkasjärvi are 9.3 miles (15 kilometres) from Kiruna which has a train station and airport, both of which connect to major Swedish cities. The 'warm' section of the hotel is open year round and the cold rooms from December to April.

Further Information: For further information and to book a room visit **www.icehotel.com**. A comprehensive travel planning guide to Sweden is offered by the tourism authority **www.visitsweden.com**.

PUERTO PRINCESA
PALAWAN, PHILIPPINES

On the long, narrow island of Palawan, deep underneath the St Paul mountain range, a great river snakes its way 5 miles (8.2 kilometres) through immense limestone caverns and tunnels, the only sounds are those of the roaring water and bats flapping in the eerie darkness. A dot of light grows bigger as the river emerges into daylight, tumbling into the cobalt blue sea at its mouth. Despite being tipped from its podium as the world's longest underground river in 2007 by one found beneath Mexico's Yucatan, the Puerto Princesa is certainly the longest one that can be traversed by boat or canoe, and sits in the heart of a region so beautiful and unique it has been declared both an UNESCO World Heritage Site and one of the New 7 Wonders of Nature.

The Cabayugan River pours down the slopes of Mt. Bloomfield, irrigating the region's pretty green paddy farms before disappearing under Mt. St. Paul. Gushing underground it has gouged cavernous chambers in the limestone rocks, the vast caves – some of which measure 120 metres (393 feet) wide by 60 metres (197 feet) high – decorated by fantastical rock formations and inhabited by fish, snakes, insects and bats. As it reaches the sea the water turns brackish, and the river is subjected to the power of the tides in a unique global phenomenon. Traditional paddleboats take visitors 2.7 miles (4.3 kilometres) into the belly of the mountain, navigating the river upstream.

The river is the crowning glory of a national park gleaming with natural treasures. A complete mountain to sea ecosystem exists here, jagged mountain peaks giving way to rolling hinterlands and flat plains, dense forests and tangled mangroves before reaching the pristine clear waters of St Paul's Bay. Wildlife thrives in this kaleidoscopic landscape, endemic stink badgers and porcupines living alongside macaques and pythons, turtles and dugongs. The Batak and Tagbanua, two of Palawan's seven cultural groups, live amidst the abounding nature in their ancestral home.

Palawan is ringed by sugar-white beaches, the most secluded and unspoilt hidden within the national park's protective boundaries. Endangered turtles feed on the sea grass beds and nest in the warm sand, birds big and small take respite in the sanctuary created for them amidst the mangroves and freshwater swamps, and a sprinkling of idyllic tropical islands just beg to be explored. It is an outdoor enthusiast's dream, a micro-world of immaculate landscapes where mountain hiking, island-hopping, wildlife-watching, adventure caving and jungle trekking come hand in hand with venturing deep into the great underground river.

Take Me There

How to Visit: Puerto Princesa city acts as the gateway to the national park from where tours can be arranged. It is two hours drive to the town of Sabang near the park entrance. The city has daily flights from Manila. Alternatively there are eco-lodges near the park and in Sabang.

Further Information: Visit the official park website **www.puerto-undergroundriver.com** for regional information, and for travel information to the Philippines the national tourism **itsmorefuninthephilippines.com** and Palawan **www.palawan.gov.ph** websites.

Did You Know?

Palawan is an archipelago made up of 1,780 islands and islets. The country with the most islands is Indonesia with 17,000, only 6,000 of which are inhabited. Together with the Philippines' 7,000 islands the two countries form the Malay Archipelago, the largest group of islands in the world.

BOROBUDUR
INDONESIA

As the sun rises slowly behind Mount Merapi volcano an orange glow creeps across the valley of the Kedu Plain, swirling with the dense morning mist to create an ethereal and theatrical glow. As it spreads light across the great, raised stage, the sheer size and intricacy of Borobudur temple is revealed in all its glory. For the world's largest Buddhist temple is colossal, a vast pyramid perched atop a hill towering into the sky, woven with delicate stone carvings and watched over by more than 500 serene Buddhas.

For 500 years Borobudur lay abandoned, engulfed by a layer of volcanic ash and a dense tangle of vegetation, its sudden desertion in the 14th century a mystery to this day. It was built half a century before, during the reign of the Sailendra Dynasty in the 9th century – 300 years before Cambodia's Angkor Wat came to being – but was left to the ravages of nature with the arrival of Islam in Java. It wasn't until 1814 that Borobudur was brought out of its long hibernation when Sir Thomas Stamford Raffles, the British ruler of Java, brought it to the world's attention. Several restorations, including the most major in 1975 by the Indonesian government and UNESCO, has returned Borobudur to its gleaming former glory, and pilgrims once again flock here annually, during the height of the full moon, to celebrate Vesak (often known as Buddha Day) making the temple the most visited site in Indonesia.

Climbing all the way up Borobudur is a pilgrimage in itself, the pyramidal temple guiding the faithful from one symbolic level to another on the ultimate journey to enlightenment. Built from two million dark grey andesite blocks, stones gathered 1200 years ago from nearby rivers and streams, the temple stands 29 metres (95 feet) high, six massive square platforms topped by a further three round ones taking the form of the Buddhist Mandala. Over 3,000 bas-reliefs – a melding of Indonesian and Indian forms – have been carved into the walls and balustrades of the shrine making this the largest collection of Buddhist sculpture on the planet.

Visiting Borobudur is a spiritual and reflective experience. Those that embark on the herculean climb to its summit pass through three levels of symbolic Buddhist cosmology on their way to Nirvana (unconsciousness), represented by a massive bell-shaped stupa 10 metres (33 feet) in diameter. In its higher terraces, 72 open stupas, each containing a statue of Buddha, gaze across the sweeping valley, where rivers meander and the two other temples of Pawon and Mendut form a perfect line with Borobudur in this ancient and sacred landscape.

Did You Know?

Indonesia is home to the largest flowering plant on earth, *Rafflesia Arnoldi*. Measuring a metre (3.3 feet) in width and weighing 11 kilograms (24 pounds) its unmistakable smell has been compared to rotting flesh awarding it the nickname 'the corpse flower'.

Take Me There

How to Visit: Borobudur is 25 miles (40 kilometres) from Yogyakarta, from where day tours can be booked. Alternatively, you can stay in Borobudur village near the park entrance and visit independently.

Further Information: Information on visiting the temple can be found on the official website **www.borobudurpark.com** while the tourism website **www.indonesia.travel** offers more general information on visiting Indonesia.

HIGH COAST SWEDEN
KVARKEN ARCHIPELAGO FINLAND

The shifting landscape of Sweden's High Coast and Finland's Kvarken Archipelago – together an UNESCO World Heritage Site – is one of the planet's most fascinating geological phenomena; for the land is growing. Islands are appearing from the Gulf of Bothnia between the two countries, others are merging together. Bays are becoming separated from the sea, forming small lakes or brackish wetlands. It is a strange process known as post-glacial rebound, which affects northern Europe, Siberia, Canada and the northern United States. Yet nowhere is it more pronounced and dramatic than in this wild and vastly untouched region of Sweden and Finland.

Around 20,000 years ago huge ice sheets covered northern swathes of the world, their enormity and crushing weight squashing the land beneath it – above the Kvarken and High Coast the ice sheet measured 1.8 miles (3 kilometres) thick in parts. At the end of the Ice Age the land sprung back up quickly, a process that continues to this day. Rising at a speed of 80 centimetres (31 inches) a year results in 0.6 square miles (one square kilometre) of new land popping up from the surface of the water – the size of 150 football pitches. At this rate, in 2,000 years' time, Finland and Sweden will be joined not by a brackish arm of the Baltic Sea but by land.

The two sides of the gulf couldn't look more different, despite the same geological processes at play. Sweden's High Coast is precisely that, a hilly shore fringed by tall islands, narrow deep bays and smooth cliffs. Across the channel Finland's Kvarken Archipelago is a flat mosaic of low-lying islands, shallow bays and boulder and moraine fields left behind by retreating glaciers.

Both regions are spell-binding places to visit. The Skuleskogen National Park sits in the heart of Sweden's 62 miles- (100 kilometre) long High Coast, offering woodland hiking and biking trails voted the country's best many times over. Summertime boats weave between the islands and fishing villages, and safaris take you in search of bears and beavers. Horse-ride along the rocky shoreline, go in search of waterfalls and caves, or trek 286 metres (938 feet) up the cliffs to meet the waterline of 10,000 years ago.

Hiking and cycling are also top pursuits on the barren Kvarken Archipelago. You can explore the hundreds of rounded islands by canoe, set sail in the strong winds that whip across the gulf, or bird-watch in quiet contemplation of an ever-changing landscape. At the end of the day, relax in a wooden guesthouse and soak in a wood-fired sauna in true Finnish style. No-one knows precisely for how long the land will continue to rise, but make a return visit to the region in a few years and there will be plenty of new places waiting to be discovered.

Take Me There

How to Visit: Both countries offer plentiful accommodation including cabins, camping and guesthouses in a number of fishing villages – all listed on the tourism authority websites. Domestic airports connect to the capitals and there are efficient public transport networks.

Further Information: Excellent guides are provided by the regional www.highcoastsweden.com; www.kvarkenworldheritage.fi and national www.visitfinland. com; www.visitsweden.com tourism authorities.

Did You Know?

The sleepy fishing village of Skeppsmalen along Sweden's High Coast is home to the world's only herring museum, dedicated to the regional specialty of Surströmming (fermented herring). The smell is so strong that it has to be eaten outdoors.

THE CANTON TOWER
GUANGZHOU, CHINA

The Canton Tower is a vertigo sufferer's worst nightmare. It would be understandable to assume that the 350 metre (1,148 feet) high open stairwell that snakes around the narrow building is as terrifying as it gets, but that doesn't even come close to what the tower has up its sleeve. It's not even the glass-floored viewing boxes that pop out of the sides, giving uninterrupted views hundreds of metres down to Guangzhou's busy streets. At least they're enclosed. It's at the top of the 450 metre (1,476 feet) high main section of the building (there's a further 150 metre-(492 feet) long antenna on top of it) that palms really begin to sweat, when visitors step into glass bubbles to be taken on a top-of-the-world horizontal ferris wheel ride. Go one step further and you arrive at 488 Lookout, the Canton Tower's record-breaking trump card; an outdoor observation deck 488 metres (1,601feet) above the sprawling metropolis below.

Few could argue that the Dutch architects of the Canton Tower failed in their mission to make an elegant and feminine-looking building, her slim waist and gentle curves having awarded her the nickname 'the supermodel' or 'Xiao Man's waist' after one of China's most famous geishas. When it was opened in October 2010 it was Guangzhou's crowning glory of the 16th Asian Games which they hosted, and shot into the record books not as the fifth largest freestanding building on the planet, but as having the highest outdoor observation deck.

While the interior of the building is home to TV and radio transmission facilities (one of the building's main raison d'être), exhibition spaces, conference rooms, two suave revolving restaurants, shops and even the world's highest 4-D cinema, it's what's on the outside that really gets the heart pumping. Towering over the neon-flashing, bustling city below the tower offers almost as many ways to feel your heart in your mouth as the city below has restaurants – incidentally, Guanzhou has more restaurants per capita than any other Chinese city. Outdoor gardens complete with teahouses hang off the 'lower' echelons of the building, guided tours up the Skywalk staircase spiral 200 metres (656 feet) up through the infrastructure of the edifice, and 16 transparent capsules take 40 minutes to circumnavigate the perimeter through clouds and mist. For the true daredevils there is the Sky Drop, a terrifying ride that plummets screaming participants from 485 to 455 meters (1,591 to 1,492 feet) in a single heart-in-mouth fall. And all this before you even step foot on the platform at the very top, from where you look down on the skyscrapers and high rises, the city's Pearl River appearing stream-sized in the distance.

Did You Know?

The architectural design of the Canton Tower was patented by the Russian architect Vladimir Shukhov in 1899. In 1920 he designed the Adziogol Lighthouse in Ukraine's Dnepr Delta. The structures of both buildings are strikingly similar.

Take Me There

How to Visit: The tower is located in the heart of Guangzhou and is widely accessible by public transport (there is a metro station inside the building). The city is served by an international airport.

Further Information: For more information about the construction and facilities available in the Canton Tower visit **www.cantontower.com**.

FRASER ISLAND
AUSTRALIA

The Aborigines know it as K'Gari, meaning 'Paradise', a name which captures the very essence of the great 1,143 square miles (1,840 square kilometre) island in a single word. For despite being the largest sand island on the planet, Fraser Island is far from a barren and inhospitable desert. Here, the world's only sand-growing rainforest blankets the shores of crystal clear creeks and over 100 freshwater lakes support a kaleidoscope of bird and wildlife. Towering multi-coloured sand dunes – up to 240 metres (787 feet) tall – roll along a coast ringed by white sand beaches and lapped by turquoise waters.

Like a floating oasis, the giant sand spit of Fraser Island sits just off the Queensland coast, its past as colourful as the sand dunes for which it is famous. A 5,000-year-old aboriginal ancestry, timber pioneers and tales of shipwrecked survivors have left a long legacy and indelible mark on the island – the rusting hulk of the ship wreck *SS Maheno* has become one of Fraser's icons. She met her end in 1935 en route to Japan, the red brown carcass today buried in the fine quartz sand. Thick eucalyptus woodlands, tangled mangrove forests and heaths cloaked in spring wildflowers have created a varied utopia for wildlife, where wallabies, possums, bandicoots and flying foxes live alongside snakes, butterflies and over 350 species of rainbow-coloured birds – eagles, falcons, yellow-crested cockatoos and the endangered Eastern Ground Parrot amongst them. In the sea, humpback whales and dolphins, dugongs and turtles, saltwater crocodiles and tiger, bull and great white sharks gorge on the plentiful fish. Despite the wonderful wildlife-spotting opportunities, the highlight on many a visitors' animal bucket list is the increasingly rare wild dingo – believed to be some of the last remaining pure dingoes in Australia.

Nature-lovers flock to Fraser in their thousands, the island swallowing them up amidst the expansive wild landscape. This is a place where roads are virtually non-existent, and planes vie for landing space on Seventy Five Mile Beach, which doubles as a natural highway for four wheel drive vehicles. It is a place where the lakes can be as clear as water or a deep tea-red. To fully experience Fraser Island, set off on a bushwalk through the tropical rainforest in search of wildlife, hike the sand tracks and boardwalks that crisscross the island, picnic at Lake Allom where freshwater turtles lounge on the shore, or watch the sun set behind the *Maheno* wreck. Wade through the cascades at Rainbow Gorge, hire a jeep and fly down the beach road, trek the Lake McKenzie Circuit Walk or kayak and swim the blue seas.

Did You Know?

The Anna Creek Station in South Australia is the largest cattle station in the world. At over 21,126 miles (34,000 square kilometres) it is bigger than Belgium.

Take Me There

How to Visit: Fraser Island can be reached by ferry or chartered flight from the mainland. Inter-island transport is by private-hire four wheel drive, and accommodation ranges from eco-friendly resorts to cabins, beach houses and camping.

Further Information: Travel guides are provided by the regional **www.visitfrasercoast.com** and national **www.australia.com** tourism websites, and for further ecological and cultural information visit UNESCO **whc.unesco.org**.

THE SCHÖNBRUNN ZOO
VIENNA, AUSTRIA

The Schönbrunn Palace stands regally at the head of acres of sweeping, immaculate grounds, the carpets of flowers, flawless lawns and delicate fountains as exquisite as the crystal chandeliers, gold-leaf décor and antiques that adorn its 1,441 rooms. For centuries it was the summer residence of the Hapsburg monarchs, the majestic Baroque palace having been the birthplace of Emperor Franz Joseph and the grand home of Maria Theresia – the only female ruler of the Habsburg Empire. Today, while the Austrian government gives elaborate, star-studded state receptions in the Grand Gallery, the only permanent inhabitants of Austria's most famous palace complex are 500 animal species who reside in what is the world's oldest zoo.

The zoo started life as an imperial menagerie, a flight of fancy for the then Holy Roman Emperor, Franz I (Maria Theresia's husband) who entertained his royal guests with the exotic creatures he collected from around the world. It opened to the public a few years later and, despite tumultuous years during the first and second world wars, has remained in operation for almost three centuries.

Today it is a proud centre for conservation, from early beginnings in 1906 when the first baby African elephant was conceived in captivity, until 100 years later when its status was cemented with the birth of the first giant panda to be conceived naturally in a zoo, triggering a flood of visitors – over two million people now visit every year. There are 160 hectares of pavilions and enclosures, the preserved buildings from the baroque era giving a charming sense of the 18th century menagerie. Amidst the magnificent Gloriette pavilion and swirling hedge maze, hundreds of different species live in the shadow of the grand palace; Siberian tigers and orangutans, cheetahs and sea lions, Arctic wolves and polar bears – the zoo's newest residents which can be viewed swimming gracefully underwater in their 1,700 square metre (5,577 square feet) enclosure.

With a scientific backbone centred on education, the zoo offers guided themed tours which provide a unique insight into its exotic animals. Get up close with the giants – the elephants, rhinos and hippos – or observe young animals and their mothers. Embark on an African safari, explore the bizarre creatures of the desert landscapes, or head into the zoo at night to encounter the nocturnal residents. Immerse yourself in the Amazon as you wander through the mist-shrouded rainforest house, or wander the nature trail to discover Austria's own native species; trout, carp and pike, woodpeckers, great tits, and poisonous snakes.

Did You Know?

The Schönbrunn Palace is one of Austria's most important cultural monuments and its most visited sight. In addition to its royal inhabitants, a six-year-old Mozart played a concert in the Hall of Mirrors, Napoleon met with his generals in the Vieux Laque Room and, in the Blue Chinese Salon, Emperor Charles I signed his abdication in 1918 marking the end of the Habsburg dominion.

Take Me There

How to Visit: The Schönbrunn Palace and Zoo are easily accessed from Vienna city centre by tram, bus, and park and ride.

Further Information: The official websites provide visitor information for the Schönbrunn Zoo www.zoovienna.at and Schönbrunn Palace www.schoenbrunn.at.
For travel information to Vienna, including accommodation, visit www.wien.info.

GENERAL SHERMAN
SEQUOIA NATIONAL PARK, CALIFORNIA, USA

When a tree (or branch) falls in the forest and no-one is around to hear it, does it still make a noise? When the tree is General Sherman – the world's largest tree – you can be certain that when he sheds one of his enormous branches the answer to the famous question will be a ground-shaking yes. At a towering 83.8 metres- (274.9 feet) tall General Sherman isn't the tallest tree on earth, and with a vast girth of 24.10 metres (79 feet) it isn't the widest either, but it is the biggest by volume, with a solid trunk of 1,486 cubic meters (52,500 cubic feet) of dense, hard sequoia wood – that's enough wood to make over 5 billion matches.

For thousands of years the Sequoia National Park's famous trees have stood on the slopes of California's Sierra Nevada mountains, in their midst the largest and most stout of them all, General Sherman, so named after the American Civil War general, William Tecumseh Sherman. It's reddish brown bark, thick canopy of branches and deep tangle of anchoring roots together weigh an estimated 1,814 tonnes, its first branch not bursting out until 40 metres (130 feet) up the great trunk. To stand and look up is a dizzying and humbling sight as all around the Giant Forest these behemoth's tower into the sky. Indeed, five of the ten most massive trees on earth live here, in one of the wildest stretches of North America.

While the trees might be the prime attraction, Sequoia National Park and its neighbouring Kings Canyon National Park are a backcountry playground of deep canyons, roaring rivers, cascading waterfalls, still lakes and the stately mountains of the Sierra Nevada, Mount Whitney looming above them all as the highest peak in the lower 48 states. There is a rugged splendour to the region, a place with 800 miles (1,287 kilometres) of remote trails, where you can hike the furthest from a road anywhere in the United States south of Alaska.

Steep and twisting roads lead to the Giant Forest, itself home to 40 miles (64 kilometres) of trails that weave through the groves. On General Sherman's doorstep the great granite dome of Moro Rock affords eagles nest-views over the canyon of Middle Fork, wildflowers grow in Crescent Meadow and the fallen sequoia known as Tunnel Log is big enough to drive a car through. In the summer months horse-ride through the meadows and streams, trek the mountains, fly-fish in the cool rivers or rock climb the precipitous canyons, all the while keeping an eye out for Mule deer, black bears and Peregrine falcons. In winter swap hiking boots for skis or snow-shoes and set off into the stark white landscape where snowy cross-country trails await and icy paths just beg to be tobogganed.

Did You Know?

Even though California's state flag has a brown bear on it, grizzlies haven't roamed the wilds of California since 1922 when the last bear in the state was shot just outside of Kings Canyon National Park.

Take Me There

How to Visit: General Sherman is located in Giant Forest, Sequoia National Park, California and can be reached from Fresno or Visalia. Accommodation options in the park range from camping to lodges.

Further Information: Detailed visitor information can be found on the National Park Service website **www.nps.gov/seki**.

KOLUKKUMALAI
KERALA, INDIA

Everywhere you look in this hilly green corner of India a sea of tea sways before your eyes, rolling interminably into the distance. Row upon row of luscious emerald-green coloured plants rise over the West Ghat hills, fed by the life-giving annual monsoon rains. At 2,407 metres (7,900 feet) above sea level, Kerala's Kolukkumalai is the world's highest plantation, a vast leafy ocean steeped in decades-old tea-growing traditions.

At the very southern tip of India, Kerala is one of the country's richest tea producing regions, the warm humid climate ideal for growing the globally-popular ancient Chinese plant so famously introduced to India by British colonialists. At the end of the West Ghat hills, on the fold between Kerala and the great plains of neighbouring Tamil Nadu, dozens of seemingly endless plantations blanket the landscape where not only tea but coffee and cardamom grow amongst lakes, streams and waterfalls.

The Kolukkumalai Tea Estate is not only high but remote, the sheer effort of getting there adding to the staggering beauty of the mountaintop panoramic views. By foot or painstakingly slow jeep, the route winds up and over the rudimentary road to the old tea factory built eight decades ago by British colonialists who were lured to the region in search of respite from the soaring coastal temperatures. Here the days are refreshingly crisp, and the sun shines brightly in a blue cloudless sky. Some four square kilometres (1,000 acres) of hedges stretch away from the 1930s building which is infused with old world charm and the scent of fresh tea. A thirst-quenching 144,000 kilograms (158 tonnes) of tea is produced each year from over half a million kilos (550 tonnes) of raw tea leaves – collected almost wholly by hand. For at Kolokkumalai the production processes are as organic as the tea, and traditional techniques and machinery wither, roll, sieve, ferment and dry the raw leaves into dried infusions ready to be brewed. Wandering amidst the green hedges and steep pathways the views of far away, mist-shrouded hills are breathtaking, and the sunsets create a magical hue of oranges and pinks across the sky.

While the colonial hill station of Munnar isn't the big attraction in the region, it is the jumping off point to the national parks and tea plantations of the West Ghat, including Kolokkumalai, and the town's Tea Museum tells the story of the little plant that has shaped empires. Munnar is enveloped by towering peaks – the highest in the region is the craggy Ana Mudi at 2695 metres (8,841 feet) – and forests and grasslands which once every 12 years are blanketed by the exotic blue Neelakurinji plant. Waterfalls can be hiked to, mountain peaks can be trekked up and everywhere in between simply savour the sights and flavours of India's long tea legacy.

Did You Know?

There are hundreds of different types of tea but all come from the same plant: Camellia sinensis. The colour and flavour of the tea depends on the way the tea leaves are processed once picked.

Take Me There

How to Visit: The nearest town to Kolukkumulai is Munnar from where treks and jeep tours depart. Munnar itself is accessible from Madurai International Airport and by public transport from Kochi and Aluva. There is a variety of accommodation options in the town.

Further Information: Kerala Tourism www.keralatourism. org is the best resource for planning trips to the region.

LAKE TURKANA
KENYA

There is the part of Kenya with which we are all familiar – the Maasai Mara grasslands, great wildebeest migrations and incredible wildlife safaris. And then there is Lake Turkana, a vast ethereal-looking body of water sitting in a stark, wild landscape whose shores are inhabited by semi-nomadic tribespeople and some of Africa's fiercest wildlife. In the northern stretches of the country, hugging the border with Ethiopia, Lake Turkana – often known as the Jade Sea – sits in the midst of the hot, dry and remote Chalbi Desert. At 155 miles- (250 kilometres) long it is the world's largest desert lake, an oasis which stretches longer than the entire Kenyan coast.

Some of Africa's worst and most rudimentary roads lead through a volcanic, moon-like landscape towards Lake Turkana, passing camel-herding tribes, rocky mountain deserts splattered with dried lava, and seasonal grasslands grazed by zebra, oryx, gazelle and giraffe. It is a mesmerising, untamed and sparsely inhabited part of the planet where life struggles in the arid heat. The lake is a lifeline, albeit a very salty one, its algae-rich waters shining alternately bright turquoise or brooding grey and frequent violent storms whip white peaks onto the waves that crash against the sandy beaches. Hundreds of birds live in or migrate past Turkana, including pink flamingos and pelicans, and the alkaline water manages to support populations of giant-sized Nile perch – some have been known to weigh up to 100 kilograms (220 pounds). Nile crocodiles also come super-sized in the Jade Sea, where some of the world's largest populations, containing some of the world's biggest specimens laze under the hot sun on the lakeside flats. One of the most croc-abundant waters are around Central Island, where an active triple volcano puffs vapours into the air like a scene from *Jurassic Park*.

While the lake's reptilian residents (and their fellow hippopotamuses) are undoubtedly unique, it is the human inhabitants that truly give Turkana its vitality. The lake was named after the Turkana tribe, who live a semi-nomadic lifestyle of cattle herding and fishing along the windswept beaches. The nomadic Gabra herd their camels through the Chalbi Desert, their distinctive traditional tents made from acacia roots and camel hides, while the smallest of Kenya's tribes, the El Molo, are hunter-gatherers living on the lake's shores in rounded reed huts.

Visitors to the region come in search of an Africa untouched by tourism, where hardy four wheel drives bounce along rocky roads and camps are pitched on the windy shores. It is a chance to discover a traditional and hospitable people who harness the wild landscape as they have done for centuries, and to step foot in a prehistoric land unchanged by the trappings of modern times.

Did You Know?

Prehistoric remains recovered from the shores of Lake Turkana are some of the earliest remains of human ancestors found anywhere in the world, and have given huge insight into the evolution of man.

Take Me There

How to Visit: Visiting Lake Turkana independently is difficult and most visit as part of an organised expedition lasting around 10 days and departing from Nairobi.

Further Information: For travel advice, visit the Kenya tourism website **www.magicalkenya.com** which lists both national and international reputable tour operators.

BURJ KHALIFA
DUBAI

Dubai's Burj Khalifa towers like a glinting silver-plated rocket into the sky, leaving the once self-respecting sky rises which surround it with serious inferiority complexes. At 828 metres (2,716.5 feet) high, the building is enormous, not just dominating the skyline of the cosmopolitan city but taking the full limelight, like a prima donna under the spotlight of the hot desert sun.

It is one of the world's great engineering masterpieces, dwarfing all others that once proudly held world records; it is the tallest free-standing structure, a record previously held by Toronto's CN Tower, and also the tallest structure, an accolade once owned by the KVLY-TV mast in Blanchard, North Dakota. But the list of records doesn't stop there. It has the most number of floors of any building (163, plus 46 maintenance levels), the world's highest and fastest lifts, the highest restaurant (442 metres/1,450 feet) the highest mosque (158th floor) and highest swimming pool (76th floor). It even has the highest nightclub (144th floor).

The Burj Khalifa broke all the moulds when it was built in 2004, and to say that it is a revolutionary piece of architecture is no overstatement. It took 22 million hours of labour to shape 330,000 cubic metres (431,600 cubic yard) of concrete, 39,000 tonnes of steel rebar and enough aluminium to build five A380 airplanes into the glass-fronted, triangular-shaped building. And just how do they clean all those windows over half a kilometre above the streets below? Using state-of-the-art, retractable maintenance units – and it still takes four months to clean all 120,000 square metres (1,290,000 square feet) of glass.

The majority of the building's mini city has been given over to 900 residential properties – which sold out within hours of coming on the market. Luxury facilities are aplenty; top-of-the-world swimming pools, a four-storey fitness and recreation suite and fine dining restaurant. In the lower floors, Giorgio Armani was let loose designing the world's first Armani Hotel – a blend of elegance, opulence and classic hospitality – complete with no less than eight restaurants. Corporate suites reside in the dizzying high floors, and right at the top, memorably-named 'At the Top', is the observation deck. Perched 124 metres (406 feet) above the glamorous, futuristic-looking city below it offers views that stretch from the white sand of the beaches to the white sand of the desert.

The Burj Khalifa has changed Dubai, the silver needle firing heavenwards above the ultra-fashionable shopping streets, state-of-the-art infrastructure and millionaire's mansions. To fully comprehend the magnitude of the building you're best to view it from afar – it is a shining testament to the capabilities of mankind.

Did You Know?

Dubai is also home to the world's largest man-made island, Palm Island. Made from sand and rocks the island radiates out into the sea in the shape of palm fronds and is home to luxury hotels and prime real estate.

Take Me There

How to Visit: Dubai's International Airport is a major transport hub and widely accessible from around the world. The building has many leisure facilities for visitors.

Further Information: The website for the Burj Khalifa **www.burjkhalifa.ae** contains lots of interesting information, while the official Dubai tourism website **www.definitelydubai.com** is a good source for planning a trip to the city.

THE SUNDARBANS
BANGLADESH/INDIA

There is a wonderful sense of irony in two of the world's most densely inhabited countries – India and Bangladesh – being home to one of the wildest, most remote and truly feral stretches of land on the planet. Extending 160 miles (260 kilometres) along the vast delta of the Bay of Bengal, and reaching inland for up to 50 miles (80 kilometres), the Sundarbans is an impenetrable tangle of forests, estuaries, swamps, great tidal rivers and winding creeks. As they reach the shore the forests turn to coastal mangroves – the largest in the world – where sand dunes emerge from mist-covered mudflats, and marshy islands are formed in the spaghetti-like maze of channels and rivers.

The Sundarbans is a complex ecosystem, an area measuring 3,860 square miles (10,000 square kilometres) which supports life from the tiniest of shrimps that thrive in the tidal swamps, to the majestic Royal Bengal Tigers that prowl the mangrove forests hunting for Chital deer, wild boars and Rhesus Macaques. Here, the land and rivers melt into the sea, creating the ideal habitats for over 150 species of fish and crustaceans in the knotted roots, and birds, mongoose, flying foxes, snakes, jungle cats and the armadillo-esque Pangolins in the raised mangrove forests. Saltwater crocodiles, turtles and snakes saunter through the brackish water, and the freshwater rivers are home to sharks and the endangered Ganges River dolphins.

The mangroves stretch across the two countries, and it is possible to visit from either. There are no roads, but boats penetrate the primitive forests through the network of rivers which create a wild, mini-city of watery avenues. Khulna in Bangladesh is the main jumping off point for live-aboard boats into the mangroves, and within India, the Sundarbans National Park is an UNESCO World Heritage Site, Tiger Reserve and Biosphere Reserve, accessed by boat trips that ply the creeks. Multi-day trips give you time to climb the wildlife watchtowers, meet local villagers, learn to fish or catch crabs, visit the crocodile farms and bird sanctuaries, and spend quiet hours on the trail of the elusive tigers. So delve into the heart of a fierce and unforgiving region whose waters teem with all manner of weird, wonderful and somewhat dangerous creatures and experience a serenity that permeates above all else, a place where nature thrives in this wild and raw environment.

Take Me There

How to Visit: Sundarban National Park is 87 miles (140 kilometres) from Kolkata, India and has rail and road connections. Mangroves trips start from Raidighi, Najat, Sonakhali and Namkhana. In Bangladesh safaris go from Khulna accessed from Dhaka. Accommodation is either in lodges or on board.

Further Information: The West Bangal Tourism www.wbtourism.gov.in offers detailed travel information. Tour companies to choose from include:
Tour de Sundarbans www.tourdesundarbans.com and Sundarban Chalo www.sundarbanchalo.com in India, and The Guide Tours www.guidetoursbd.com and Bengal Tours www.bengaltours.com in Bangladesh.

Did You Know?

Just 500 tigers live in the Sundarbans, the biggest population in the world and a sobering reality of the endangered state of these magnificent animals. Attacks on humans – usually farmers and fishermen – are relatively common, with human deaths ranging from 30–100 per year.

SUBLIMOTION
IBIZA, SPAIN

For those in search of a relaxed evening of romance, quiet conversation and a three-course meal, then Sublimotion is probably not the place to go. If however, it's a multi-sensory meal of twenty fantastical dishes served amidst a swirling, ever-changing dining hall of 360 degree projections enjoyed alongside 11 other guests, then this is just the place. The latest brainchild of famed, double Michelin-starred Spanish chef Paco Roncero is an innovative, ambitious and never-before-seen dining experience designed to stimulate the senses – we're talking flying plates, spinning toadstools and self-mixing margaritas. The price for an evening at Sublimotion however, might be the block over which many stumble – at £1200 (US$2,000) per person it is the world's most expensive restaurant.

Sublimotion is the latest accolade to grace the flamboyant, risqué Balearic island of Ibiza, a sunny little isle in the Mediterranean whose party reputation is legendary. Inconspicuously housed in the Hard Rock Ibiza Hotel, it's not the sort of place you encounter on an evening stroll – there are no windows and nicely laid tables offering sea views. Deep within the hotel and 'down' a simulated disco lift, the dining room is stark, white and empty. Emblazoned in lights across a large blank table are the guest's names and, after taking their seats, Paco and his team unleash the full force of their culinary and imaginative creativity upon them.

It is an evening of pure theatre where emotions are stirred and senses tickled as the room is transformed into an all-encompassing cinema. As each dish is served amidst a flurry of eccentricity, diners are transported on a journey from the North Pole – where they carve their own dish from an iceberg placed theatrically in front of them – to the baroque Versailles, where butterflies dart across the table and vines weave up the walls as diners are presented with an intricate rose dish. It is the blending of culinary art and technological innovation, where each mouthful is accentuated and enhanced with temperature, humidity and music.

From a foie gras doughnut that enters the room by balloon (and which is eaten under the sea) to levitating, spinning macaroons, there are unexpected turns throughout the evening. Nitrogen-frozen olive oil parcels hang on a mini washing line complete with wooden pegs, and liquid hydrogen mystically floats out of most dishes. There are test tubes of margarita ingredients, rich liquid cheese, journeys to ancient libraries and fiery hells. It is a two and a half hour spectacle which evokes a myriad of senses; laughter, pleasure, trepidation, reflection and nostalgia, but also a childlike excitement, like Charlie and the Chocolate Factory for affluent grown-ups.

Did You Know?

The world's largest permanent light and sound show is Hong Kong's Symphony of Lights. Every evening over 40 buildings on either side of the harbour perform a dance of coloured lights, laser beams and searchlights synchronised to music.

Take Me There

How to Visit: Ibiza is one of Europe's top destinations and there are many airlines serving the island, especially in summer. Accommodation options vary widely from hotels to luxury private villas.

Further Information: For contact information and to make a reservation visit www.sublimotionibiza.com. The Hard Rock Hotel Ibiza www.hrhibiza.com and local tourism authority www.ibiza.travel provide further travel advice and accommodation options.

THE ATACAMA DESERT
CHILE/BOLIVIA

In the foothills of South America's Andes Mountains, a strip of desert runs along the Pacific coast of northern Chile, Bolivia and into Peru. Stretching 600 miles (965 kilometres) across the plateau at an average 4,000 metres (13,123 feet) above sea level it is the highest desert in the world, a harsh and inhospitable environment, where the blistering sun shines in a cloudless sky and fierce winds whip past towering peaks and puffing volcanoes. In the heart of the Atacama Desert there are places which researchers believe haven't seen rainfall for four centuries, with others receiving just 10 centimetres (3 inches) of rain every 1,000 years – making this also the driest inhabited place in the world. The heart of the Atacama is so arid the mountains are glacier-free and not a blade of grass or even a resilient cactus grows here – although the fringes of the desert are home to some hardy and well-adapted flora and fauna.

The landscape is bizarre, fantastical and more reminiscent of Mars than anywhere on planet Earth. Hollywood movies such as *Space Odyssey* were filmed in the red, dusty Valley of the Moon, NASA scientists and their Mars explorers are frequent visitors, and astronomers take advantage of the 300 clear nights a year. Wisps of smoke drift out of perfectly conical volcanoes, steaming geysers bubble, and lakes of red, green and powder blue play tricks on the eye. Only the hardiest of desert-dwellers can withstand life in this arid, barren plateau. Headdress-toting alpacas brave the unforgiving weather, majestic condors soar overhead and Andean flamingos seek warmth in the steaming thermal pools.

At 2,400 metres (7,874 feet) above sea level San Pedro de Atacama is, quite literally, the breathtaking gateway to the region, the city's reputation as a far-flung outpost long forgotten as it embraces its status as one of Chile's top tourist destinations. From here you can choose between one- or multi-day trips into the desert. From the small town of Tupiza, Bolivia set off in the footsteps of the infamous outlaws Butch Cassidy and the Sundance Kid who, as legend has it, met their grizzly end in the dusty, wrinkled, cactus-ridden hills north of town. So wrap up warm, take some lip balm and embark on an adventure into an arid world of bizarre, wind-sculpted rock formations, great sand dunes and oozing mud pools.

Did You Know?

Without moisture, nothing decays and the arid soil of the Atacama Desert is a wonderful preserver of anything unlucky enough to get lost and die within it. The museum of Padre Le Paige in San Pedro de Atacama is home to perfectly preserved mummies discovered near the Peru border. With the oldest dating to 6,000BC – 2,000 years older than Egyptian mummies – they are the oldest artificially mummified remains in the world.

Take Me There

How to Visit: One of the best bases for exploring the desert is San Pedro de Atacama, Chile whose nearest airport is Calama. There are regular flights from Santiago and nearby border crossings from Argentina and Bolivia. Another gateway is Tupiza, Bolivia. Excursions are by organised tour.

Further Information: www.visitchile.com provides information on tour companies heading into the desert. Several companies offer 4-day tours from Tupiza to Uyuni in Bolivia including Tupiza Tours **www.tupizatours.com**.

ULM MINSTER
GERMANY

The city of Ulm has two claims to fame (three if you count it being the home of the world's most crooked house). Firstly it was the birthplace of Albert Einstein, although he only lived in the city for the first year of his life. The second is hard to miss as it towers over the buildings and Danube River below – the world's tallest church. Like a great Gothic finger pointing heavenwards the steeple of Ulm Minster (or Ulmer Münster in German) rockets 161 metres (528 feet) into the air.

Ulm Minster started life in the 14th century as Roman Catholic, but during the Reformation in 1530, when the congregation converted to Protestantism, it became Lutheran and, in 1543, work stopped abruptly on the church. For almost 300 years it stood unfinished, crumbling into ruins until work once more commenced and, when the last stone was laid in 1890, the final height topped that of the mammoth Cologne Cathedral. It is the fourth tallest structure in the world built before 1900.

The church's Gothic architecture and medieval art make it remarkably beautiful. Famous German sculptors have left their marks in the busts carved on the oak pews, in the 15th century choir stalls and in the pulpit canopy.

Stone gargoyles stare down ominously from every angle, the organ once graced the fingers of Mozart, and the largest bell, Gloriosa, weighs a staggering 4,912 kilograms (10,829 pounds). Every year at 7.15pm on 17th December Gloriosa and her 12 fellow bells chime out across the city as a memorial to the day in 1944 when Ulm was bombed. While most of the city was destroyed on that day, the church survived.

Ulm Minster does a good job of hogging the limelight and long before you arrive in the city it will capture your attention. Yet look around on ground level and the city has a distinct charm where historic and modern buildings have woven together. Wander through the medieval Marktplatz (market) at the foot of the church, home to colourful farmers' markets and festive Christmas fairs. Explore the wooden houses in the Fishermen's Quarter of the old town, or amble along the Danube River and city wall. For the best view of the city however, climb the 768 twisting spiral steps to the very top of the church for the most spectacular of panoramas. From the jumble of buildings in Old Ulm below, the view stretches out across Baden-Württemberg, into Bavaria and as far away as the Alps.

Did You Know?

Designed by the famous Catalan architect Antoni Gaudí, the Sagrada Família church is a striking Barcelona landmark. Although work began on the church in 1882 it is still not finished. By the expected completion date of 2026 – the centennial of Gaudí's death – it will overtake Ulm Minster as the tallest church in the world.

Take Me There

How to Visit: The city of Ulm can be reached by fast train services from Munich, Stuttgart and Friedrichshafen all of which have international airports. The church is open to visitors and the spire steps can be climbed outside of service times.

Further Information: A comprehensive travel guide to Ulm is provided by the official tourism website **www.germany.travel**. For further details about the church visit **www.ulmer-muenster.de** (in German).

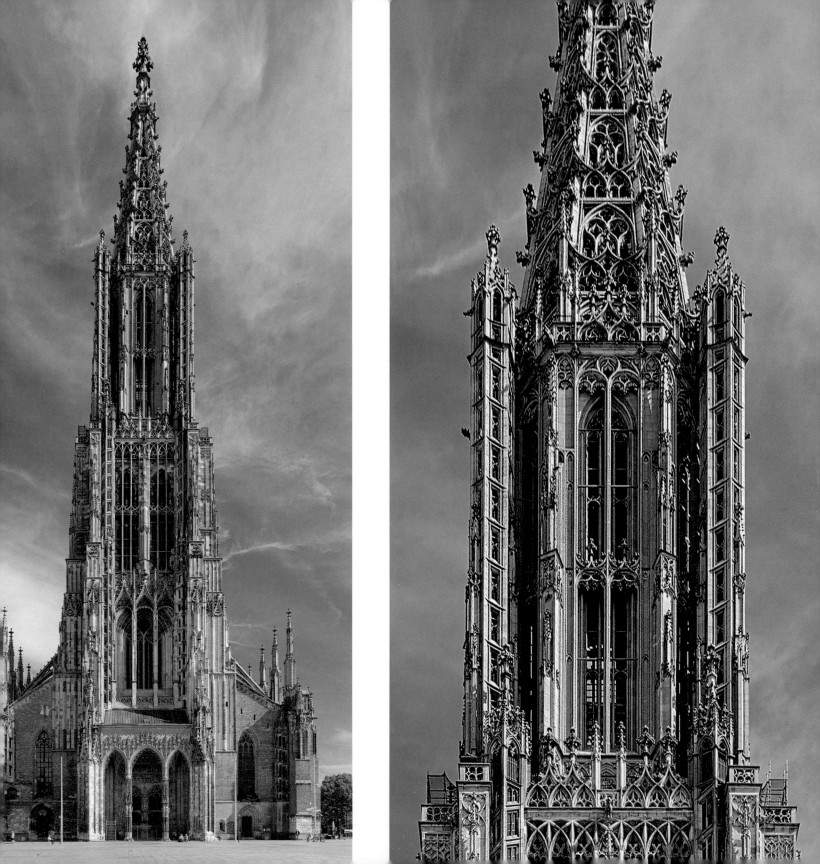

OYMYAKON
RUSSIA

There is a certain irony in the world's coldest inhabited place being called Oymyakon, meaning 'unfrozen water', so named for the thermal springs that once drew reindeer hunters to an oasis in a huge frozen desert. For here, in Russia's remote wilderness in a land known as the Sakha Republic (Yakutia), Oymyakon once measured a temperature of −71°C (−95°F). Only the uninhabited realm of Antarctica has ever recorded lower.

Life in a town where the average minimum temperature for December, January, and February is below −50°C (−58°F) is harsh and unforgiving. Cars left outside must be kept running, their inner workings no match for the claw of the cold that can shatter them in mere moments. Plumbing through the concrete-hard ground is difficult and most toilets are frost-encrusted outhouses, and bonfires are lit to thaw the ground before a funeral. Nothing can grow here, and the 500-strong population survive on reindeer and horse meat, fish from the nearby Oymyakon River and Labynkyr Lake and the one lone shop.

The town is a two day drive from the regional capital city of Yakutsk, itself laying claim to being the world's coldest city. The route heads east into the wild mountainous lands of Yakutia along the famed Kolyma Highway. Known chillingly as the 'Road of Bones' for the remains of the prisoners of Soviet gulag camps that died in its construction during the gold and diamond rush of the Stalin era, it is only traversable in winter when it stretches 1,200 miles (1,930 kilometres) to Magadan on the Pacific coast.

Sitting in a giant, bowl-like valley the cold mist settles like an icy blanket over Oymyakon, freezing everything it touches. Indeed, the town has never recorded an above-freezing temperature between October 25th and March 17th. Reindeer stand in their hundreds in a stark white landscape marked only by pointed pine trees, their boughs bending under the weight of snow. Yet for those that venture to this frigid town – and many do – is to understand a way of life like nowhere else on the planet. From ice-fishing for white salmon to visiting a Yakutian horse-breeding farm, taking a ride on a reindeer sled or partaking in the annual Pole of Cold Festival, wintry adventures await. While the summers in this far-flung corner of Russia can be warm, with temperatures spiking 30°C (86°F), it's the winter months that can freeze a breath of air as it passes the lips, a land where, should you choose to venture outside naked, will kill you in under a minute.

Did You Know?

The frozen lands of Siberia have remained untouched since the last Ice Age, and it is believed over 150 million woolly mammoths are still buried beneath the permafrost. In 2013 the best-preserved specimen of a woolly mammoth – complete with hair and flesh – was discovered by reindeer herders in Yakutia. It is estimated to be 39,000 years old.

Take Me There

How to Visit: Visiting Oymyakon isn't for the faint-hearted and good preparations must be made in advance. The town can be reached by car (tours) from Yakutsk which has flight links from Moscow and there are several guesthouses in town.

Further Information: The best source of information on visiting the region is www.askyakutia.com. Tours can be booked with Visit Yakutia www.visityakutia.com and Yakutia Travel www.yakutiatravel.com.

TYNE COT CEMETERY
BELGIUM

When King George V visited Tyne Cot Cemetery in 1922, a few short, painful years after the end of the First World War, he declared, 'I have many times asked myself whether there can be more potent advocates of peace upon Earth through the years to come, than this massed multitude of silent witnesses to the desolation of war.' Row upon row of bright white tombstones stretched out before him, the fresh graves of the 310,000 men who lost their lives in the Battle of Passchendaele. For here, in the green hills of Flanders, lies the world's largest allied cemetery, the final resting place of the Commonwealth forces which fought in one of the most contentious and bloody battles in history.

Of the 11,954 graves, 8,367 are unidentified and unnamed, marked by clean white tombstones, manicured lawns and pale pink roses winding between them. At the far end, a sweeping memorial stands proudly, guarded on each end by kneeling angels and domed rotundas. The great wall is engraved with the names of 34,927 missing soldiers who have no known grave – one of four memorials to the missing in this region known as the Ypres Salient.

Few battles encapsulate the First World War better than the Battle of Passchendaele, often known as the Battle of Mud for the relentless rains – the worst in 30 years – that turned the green fields into a quagmire, battering troops, immobilising tanks and drowning soldiers and horses. With the German submarine bases on the coast of Belgium as their target, the Western Front inched across the flat plains of Flanders, both sides suffering catastrophic losses. Three months of stalemate ensued and, after a final battle, the allies eventually captured what little remained of Passchendaele village on 6th November 1917. They had moved just 5 miles.

At the heart of the cemetery stands the Cross of Sacrifice, built on the original German blockhouse which was captured by the 3rd Australian Division on 4th October 1917. It was used as an advanced dressing station and battlefield graveyard throughout the offensive, and was greatly enlarged after the Armistice when remains were brought in from the surrounding battlefields. Today Tyne Cot is more than a peaceful final home to the troops who died. It stands as a symbol of remembrance, the nearby Memorial Museum of Passchendaele 1917 set in the historical castle of Zonnebeke providing a stark insight into the bloody offensive that claimed almost half a million lives.

Did You Know?

The Victoria Cross is the highest military decoration awarded for bravery to members of the armed forces of Commonwealth countries, taking precedence over all other orders, decorations and medals. It is presented to the recipient or their next of kin by the British monarch at Buckingham Palace. The graves of three soldiers awarded the Victoria Cross can be found at Tyne Cot.

Take Me There

How to Visit: Tyne Cot Cemetery is located about 6.8 miles (11 kilometres) north-east of Ieper town centre in Zonnebeke. From the nearby Memorial Museum Passchendaele 1917 (www.passchendaele.be) there is a 2 mile (3 kilometres) walking and cycling path to the cemetery.

Further Information: Visit Flanders www.visitflanders. co.uk has a wealth of practical information on visiting the region. For more information on visiting Tyne Cot visit the Commonwealth War Graves Commission website www.cwgc.org.

FRYING PAN LAKE
WAIMANGU VOLCANIC VALLEY, ROTORUA, NEW ZEALAND

On 10th June 1886 a massive earthquake exploded from the depths of the earth near Rotorua on New Zealand's North Island, in what has become the country's largest ever volcanic eruption. Its destruction was widespread; 100 people lost their lives, villages were destroyed and the region's most famous attraction, the Pink and White Terraces, were submerged beneath Lake Rotomahana. Yet after the devastation, a brand new and eerily beautiful geothermal landscape was left in its place – the Waimangu Volcanic Valley. Home to some of the most internationally significant features in the world it includes the largest hot spring on the planet, the aptly-named and somewhat frightening, Frying Pan Lake.

In terms of geology, the eruption of Mount Tarawera happened a mere millisecond ago, ripping the ground open along a 10 mile (17 kilometres) line and splitting the volcano in two. Lake Rotomahana exploded to 20 times its original size, engulfing everything in its path, and seven craters formed, including Frying Pan Lake. Like a giant witches' cauldron – albeit a shallow one at 5 metres (18 feet) deep – the 38,000 square metre- (125,000 square feet) lake bubbles and hisses at 43–54°C (109–129°F), steam rising ominously from its swirling surface. Its spooky neighbour, Inferno Crater Lake, holds the record for the largest geyser-like feature in the world, its geyser bursting out at the bottom of the startlingly turquoise waters. Its eerie magic happens when, precisely every 38 days, the level rises and falls in a rhythmic cycle.

The nearby town of Rotorua has long been New Zealand's hydrothermal hub, a place where there is a permanent aroma of eggy sulphur in the air, where steam hisses from the gutters and there is an unmistakable sense that something is brewing under the streets. The Maori consider this land sacred and all around the town is a wonderland of sprouting geysers, bubbling mud pools, geothermal springs and brightly coloured silica terraces. The naturally warm waters have given rise to a legion of spas.

Tours and public transport shuttle Rotorua's visitors to the Waimangu Volcanic Valley, where a circular path weaves through the lunar-like landscape. Wallabies and black swans waddle amongst the bush and hundreds of birds relish in the wildlife refuge. It is a raw and fascinating place whose volcanic features rank of international significance and, in a world older than our minds can fathom, the only geothermal system which was born on a specific date at a given time.

Did You Know?

There is an inconspicuous hill in New Zealand called 'Taumata whakatangi hangakoauau o tamatea turi pukakapiki maunga horo nuku pokai whenua kitanatahu'. It translates as 'the place where Tamatea, the man with the big knees, who slid, climbed and swallowed mountains, known as 'landeater', played his flute to his loved one'. It is the longest place name in the world.

Take Me There

How to Visit: The Waimangu Volcanic Valley is 20 minutes from Rotorua, which has many tours and public transport options heading to the park. The closest international airport is in Auckland.

Further Information: Visitor information can be found on the Waimangu Volcanic Valley website www.waimangu.co.nz. For information and guides on planning a trip to New Zealand try www.newzealand.com and www.rotoruanz.com.

POTALA PALACE
LHASA, TIBET

The grand, fortress-like Potala Palace dominates Lhasa's skyline, its white and red façade managing to claim the attention from even the snow-capped mountain peaks that poke out behind it. It is poised regally above the city, resting atop a rocky hill higher even than Tibet's capital which is 3,700 metres (12,140 feet) above sea level, so high that the air is thin and the icy winds biting. For centuries it was the spiritual and secular home of the Dalai Lama, however following the uprising against the Chinese in 1959 the current 14th Dalai Lama and 80,000 of his followers fled across the Himalayas to India where he remains in exile to this day. The Potala Palace, once the flourishing heart of Tibetan Buddhism, is today a museum, a handful of monks left wandering the hundreds of rooms.

A palace has stood in this place for over a thousand years, but for 300 of them the Potala was a centre of Buddhist government and worship, and home to 10 consecutive Dalai Lama, including the fifth who is attributed with its construction. All around the palace he is celebrated, and his mummified body still rests inside a vast stupa made from two tonnes of gold and encrusted with jewels. The white, lower portion of the palace came first, and was the secular seat of the Dalai Lama and the apartments of the current Buddhist leader remain as they did when he fled over 50 years ago. The fifth Dalai Lama died before his red palace – the spiritual heart of the complex – could be completed, and his monks, fearing it would be abandoned, kept his death a secret for a decade.

The palace is a spectacular architectural masterpiece towering 13 stories high. Over 1,000 rooms contain 10,000 shrines and 200,000 statues, the chapels, pagodas and tombs of past Dalai Lama adorned with ornate carvings, glittering jewels and precious votive offerings. One of the pagodas alone is decorated with 200,000 pearls. The scent of incense wafts along the maze of corridors, prayer wheels hold a million invisible fingerprints and a sense of quiet spirituality emanates throughout.

Lhasa is a place that evokes that same spirituality, a remote city ringed by mountain ranges and lakes in the heart of the Tibetan wilds. Pilgrims flock here, mingling with foreign tourists as they pray. With the opening of the Qinghai – Tibet railway in 2006, even more can now make the journey – and thousands queue daily for strict quotas of tickets – for the chance to enter a palace at the very top of the world.

Did You Know?

In Tibet, Sichuan, Qinghai and Inner Mongolia sky burials are a common funerary practice. In Vajrayana Buddhism, when a person dies and their spirit leaves, their body is no longer needed. Sky burials are considered a generous way of giving back to the earth and bodies are left atop mountains for vultures or the elements to claim.

Take Me There

How to Visit: There are daily flights to Lhasa Airport from cities around China, and the Qinghai-Tibet Railway connects to major cities. Foreign visitors require a visa to China and a special permit to enter Tibet.

Further Information: UNESCO whc.unesco.org provides detailed background information about the Potala Palace. There are many tour agencies which arrange train tickets including China Highlights **www.chinahighlights.com**.

COX'S BAZAR
BANGLADESH

Bangladesh is mighty proud of its beach, and at 78 miles (125 kilometres) long there is a lot of it to boast about. Stretching along the Bay of Bengal in the south eastern part of the country, Cox's Bazar is a vast, uninterrupted sweep of sand fringed by Buddhist temples, bustling resorts, pretty islands and wild nature reserves.

In the northern stretches of the great beach is the port town of Cox's Bazar, a long-standing favourite of holidaying locals. So named in honour of Captain Cox, an officer serving in British India in the 18th century, the town is today a bustling place where large hotels loom over the main Laboni Beach, rickshaws race around the busy streets and fully-clothed locals swim in the warm seas abiding by religious Muslim traditions.

Outside of Cox's Bazar beach life rolls by at a different pace. Vast tracts of empty sand are lapped by rolling waves, sunsets bathing them in a hue of orange and purple. Traditional fishing boats line the shore and the often 300 metre- (984 feet) wide beach is backed by undulating green hills dotted with colourful pagodas. In the Himchari National Park the monsoon season brings waterfalls that cascade through the rolling hills before tipping into the sea at the wild Inani Beach. In the Buddhist village of Ramu, craftsmen sit in open pagoda-like workshops making handmade cigars and traditional crafts, a bronze Buddha statue watching over the monasteries and houses below.

In the far south, along a finger-like peninsula that points towards neighbouring Myanmar, a scurry of activity envelopes the seaside town of Teknaf. It sits on the edge of the Teknaf Game Reserve, an 11,615 hectare expanse of dense green forest through which snakes the mighty Taf River. It was established as an Asian Elephant sanctuary and is today one of the few places in the country where they can be seen roaming in the wild. Hiking opportunities abound, where monkeys hide amongst the bamboo and grasses and cruises ply the river in search of the world's largest land mammal.

From north to south, islands harbour a laid-back, traditional way of life just off the coast of the sprawling beach. Near Cox's Bazar, Sonadia supports thick mangrove forests and oyster beds, rare conch shells decorate the beaches and fishermen dry their catches in the hot sun. In the mouth of the Naf River sits the small coral island of St Martin's, with its picture-perfect turquoise waters, white sand beaches and coconut palms. Its reef teems with marine life including endangered turtles, and the 5,500-strong population survives on fishing away from the trappings of electricity, cars and modern technology.

Did You Know?

In December 2004 over 5 million people joined hands to form a human chain 652.4 miles long (1,050 kilometres)– the world's longest – which stretched from Teknaf to Tentulia, Bangladesh as part of a peaceful political protest led by the Bangladesh Awami League.

Take Me There

How to Visit: Located 93 miles (150 kilometres) south of Chittagong, Cox's Bazar is connected by air and road with the capital Dhaka. It is recommended to use a tour guide to visit Teknaf Game Reserve.

Further Information: The tourism website **www. visitbangladesh.gov.bd** offers practical travel tips for visiting Bangladesh. There are many good tour companies in the country including Tiger Tours **www.tigertoursbd.com** and Annex Travel **www.annextravel.com**.

QINGHAI-TIBET RAILWAY
CHINA/TIBET

To journey on the world's highest railway you have to complete a health declaration form. The carriages have oxygen pumped into them, oxygen masks are supplied, and every train has a doctor on board. For the Qinghai-Tibet Railway soars across the very roof of the world at an average 4,500 metres (17.464 feet) above sea level, climbing to a maximum height of 5,072 metres (16,640 feet). It is an incredible feat of engineering that has claimed itself railway records galore, traversing some of the planet's most remote, inhospitable and beautiful terrains.

The railway begins in the ancient city of Xining in China's Qinghai Province and crosses 1,215 miles (1,956 kilometres) of harsh landscapes and indomitable mountain ranges until it reaches Lhasa, Tibet's capital. Along the way it gathers accolades with every chug; 341 miles (550 kilometres) of track run along frozen ground (the longest stretch in the world), which in turn passes through the world's most elevated tunnel (Fenghuoshan Tunnel at 4,905 metres/16,092 feet) and the longest plateau tunnel, which runs 1,686 metres (5,531 feet) through the Kunlun Mountain. It passes the highest train station on the Tanggula Pass and it cost US$3.68 billion.

In a region where temperatures drop to a crippling -35°C (–31°F) and soar to over 30°C (86°F), the frozen winter ground becomes a muddy bog in the summer months, and the thin air contains up to 40% less oxygen. Carrying oxygen supplies for each passenger the train now passes over elevated tracks and causeways, while in other areas pipes circulate liquid nitrogen to keep the ground frozen. The windows have been fitted with UV-filtering glass to protect from the sun's fierce rays in these extreme altitudes, and special corridor tunnels were created to allow the region's wildlife to migrate freely.

Lhasa, once trapped behind the Tanggula Mountains, is now accessible from cities around China. The view from the window leaves travellers breathless, a state they quickly become accustomed to on a train that travels higher than any peak in continental Europe. It traverses vast grasslands inhabited by nomadic herdsmen and three gargantuan mountain ranges, their snow-capped summits towering to 7,000 metres (23,000 feet) high. It journeys through the Kunlun Range, over the mighty Tanggula Pass and around the Nyainqentanglha mountains past windswept landscapes inhabited only by Tibetan antelopes and wild donkeys, yaks and snow leopards. The great Yangtze River starts its long journey to the sea from these high frozen peaks, huge icy lakes twinkle in the blistering sunshine and all along the route stone stupas dot the wild landscape adorned with sun-bleached prayer flags ripped ragged by the biting winds.

Take Me There

How to Visit: Trains run to Lhasa from Beijing, Chengdu, Chongqing, Guangzhou, Shanghai, Xining and Lanzhou and take approximately 48 hours. Tickets can be bought from train stations or tour agencies a few weeks before departure. Visas are needed for travel to China and a special permit to Tibet.

Further Information: There are many tour agencies which arrange train tickets including China Highlights www.chinahighlights.com and China DIY Travel www.china-diy-travel.com. Travel information to China can be found on www.travelchina.gov.cn.

Did You Know?

The Yangtze River is 3,915 miles (6,300 kilometres) long – the third longest in the world – its drainage basin covers 20% of China and it has one of the biggest hydro-electric power stations in the world, the Three Gorges Dam.

NGERULMUD
PALAU

The world's smallest capital city can be found, perhaps unsurprisingly, in one of the world's smallest countries and, at only 20 years old, one of the newest countries on earth. Ngerulmud, capital of the Pacific island nation of Palau, is home to just 400 people and is less than a decade old.

Palau is made up of over 200 forested rock islands that erupt like mushrooms from crystalline waters, sandy beaches hidden beneath the shade of the dense vegetation. They stretch for miles from the main island of Koror, the original capital and home to most of Palau's residents. As part of the fledgling country's constitution the new capital was built on the largest island of Babeldaob, and much to the pride of the 20,000 residents, a grand parliamentary complex – complete with a 12 metre- (40 foot) high dome which evokes images of Washington, D.C. – was built to the cost of US$45 million.

While the administrative capital sits proudly in its new home – the grand, white complex a stark contrast to the rustic island flavour that surrounds it – Koror forms the core of island life. In Palau right-hand drive cars tootle down the left-hand oriented roads, American-style diners alternate with Japanese sushi restaurants, and large charismatic locals try and convince sceptical foreigners to try the local delicacy of whole fruit bat. For Palau is also the world's second most overweight country.

Located in the heart of the Asia Pacific region, hundreds of miles from the nearest land, the tiny island country provides the perfect conditions for one of the world's healthiest reefs. Thriving, colourful corals swirl around the shores of the rock islands, their marine populations teeming with bounty just begging to be snorkelled, kayaked or scuba dived. Indeed, not a dive site list exists that doesn't rank Palau's Blue Corner amongst the top three sites on the planet.

While Palau and its elaborate yet miniscule capital may be isolated, remote and untamed, it is precisely these attributes that make it one of the world's last unspoilt, natural beauties. Nature, history and a proud Pacific culture thrive, and it is home to the unique phenomenon that is Jellyfish Lake, where thousands of stingless jellyfish have evolved predator-less since they were cut off from the sea millions of years ago. Scars from the ferocious Second World War battles that took place on these shores are everywhere, ship and plane wrecks buried in dark lagoons, long-forgotten bunkers and their rusted machine guns dug into the rock islands.

Did You Know?

In 2009, Palau became the first country in the world to establish an ocean shark sanctuary, making the country a top ecotourism destination. Since then the country's president has announced plans to make the entire territorial waters of Palau – an area the size of France – a 100% marine sanctuary.

Take Me There

How to Visit: Palau's Airai International Airport hosts flights from the United States via Guam, and from Asia and Europe via Manila, Seoul or Tokyo. Ngerulmud is located just a few minutes' drive from the airport and 12 miles (20 kilometres) from Koror.

Further Information: The Palau Tourism Authority website www.visit-palau.com has a wealth of travel information, while local dive centres such as Fish 'n Fins www.fishnfins.com can help you plan your activities.

KING FAHD FOUNTAIN
JEDDAH, SAUDI ARABIA

When the sun sets in the sprawling Saudi Arabian city of Jeddah, it does so in spectacular style. As the twilight hours approach, the blistering hot sun begins its descent, splashing into the Red Sea and bathing the metropolitan bustle in a hue of golden orange. It is a beautiful sight, one made even more spectacular by the towering plume of water making a graceful arc across the evening sky, tumbling in a mist of raindrops into the water below.

The King Fahd Fountain – the tallest in the world – is certainly poetic, its simple elegance and sheer size evoking all manner of romantic ideas. Yet the fountain is also an engineering masterpiece, the powerful salt water jet firing 312 metres (1,024 feet) into the air at speeds of 233 miles (375 kilometres) per hour. It was constructed between 1980 and 1983, and gifted to the city by the fountain's namesake, the initial design echoing the famous fountain of Lake Geneva. Technically, the challenges of creating a salt water fountain that could launch 1,250 litres (275 gallons) of water per second as high as the Eiffel Tower were colossal. The enormous pumps and power supply were ultimately submerged 30 metres (100 feet) under the surface of the sea housed within 7,000 tonnes of concrete in a sub-aquatic edifice the size of a five-storey building. With the great cogs of machinery heaving away under the Red Sea there is nothing but the narrow tower of water to obscure the view of the Salam Palace which sits regally on the shore. Indeed, it is only ever switched off if the usually northerly winds blow from the south, threatening the palace's delicate gardens with a spray of salt water.

As the sun sets even lower and the dry heat of the Arabian day begins to abate ever so slightly, the fountain truly comes into its own. Five hundred spotlights, each mounted on man-made islands, illuminate the jet to create a shining dagger reaching into the dark sky and turn the surrounding water a glowing green. The water hangs in the air for 15 seconds, misting the city with its spray.

The fountain can be seen, day and night, from across the sprawling city of Jeddah, the great curtain dwarfing the glinting helipad-topped sky rises, the glamorous shopping malls and the coral-built houses and traditional souks of the Old Town. The best views however are from Corniche, the 18 mile– (30 kilometre) long seaside avenue lined with modern art sculptures, picnic spots and wide sandy beach. Long off-limits to outsiders, Saudi Arabia's fledgling tourism means visiting is both doable and rewarding, offering an insight into a Middle Eastern country that is both fervently traditional and refreshingly modern.

Did You Know?

The Ka'ba in Mecca is the holiest site in Islam and every year over three million people make the pilgrimage to worship there. Land in the city of Mecca costs US$100,000 per square metre, making it the most expensive property on earth.

Take Me There

How to Visit: Jeddah's international airport is the main entry point to the country and served by many airlines. There is a wide selection of upmarket hotels and resorts. Visas must be sought for entry into Saudi Arabia.

Further Information: Information on visiting Saudi Arabia, including visa practicalities, can be found on the official tourism website **www.sauditourism.sa**.

THE CONGO RIVER
THE CONGO AND DEMOCRATIC REPUBLIC OF CONGO

The Congo River is the lifeline of Western Africa, the great watery artery as turbulent as the countries that lie on its banks. On one side is The Congo, on the other the Democratic Republic of Congo (DRC). In the lower stretches of the river their two capital cities face each other across the muddy waters – the closest two capitals in the world, united in a past marred by war and hardship. The mighty river ranks second only to the Amazon for the enormous volume of water it discharges. In some parts it stretches 9 miles (14 kilometres) wide. And at its deepest point it plummets 220 metres (721 feet) down from the tempestuous surface – the world's deepest river.

For most of its 2,920 miles (4,700 kilometres) journey the river traverses the DRC's wild, untamed Congo Rainforest, a place from where stories of cannibals and fierce beasts emerge. Little has changed since the explorer Sir Henry Morton Stanley embarked on his arduous journey along the river in the 1870's; Nomadic pygmies still hunt and forage in the depths of the jungle, and fishing pirogues (dugout canoes) still ply the waters as they have done for centuries. The striped okapi, a forest-dwelling relative of the giraffe, lives a reclusive existence in the dense foliage and hippos lounge in the shallows. The river teems with all manner of creatures including the carnivorous giant tigerfish and fierce crocodiles.

The Congo is the life force of the region where barges thunder up and down laden with copper, palm oil and coffee. Its many roaring waterfalls, long stretches of hellish rapids and more than 100 huge islands hinder movement, but ships navigate the waters from Kisangani in the east to Kinshasa in the west, crossing the equator twice on their journey downstream.

Traversing the Congo River is an adventure few will make. Indeed, governments still warn against travel to parts of DRC. Yet to embark on a journey is to experience Africa in all its glory and all its danger. Guided tours do ply the waters on epic adventures where you will meet some of the last Mbuti pygmy tribes, stare in wonderment at riversides walked by elephants, lions and rhinos, and encounter a resilient, vibrant people proud of their culture. Follow in Stanley's footsteps as you explore the lively and chaotic cities closed to the world for almost two decades. The doors are once again starting to re-open and with it hope, like the great, deep river at the heart of the country, floods in.

Did You Know?

There are plans to renovate two existing dams and build two more along the Congo River. The Grand Inga Dams would provide electricity to power the entire African continent and potentially also supply power to southern Europe. They will be the largest energy-generating dams in the world.

Take Me There

How to Visit: There are still travel advisories to parts of the Democratic Republic of Congo so check before planning a visit. Several outfits offer guided two- and three-week tours of the river which begin in Kinshasa.

Further Information: There are several operators beginning tours in different regions including Safari Guides **www.safariguides.com** and Undiscovered Destinations **www.undiscovered-destinations.com**. The book *Canoeing the Congo: The First Source-to-Sea Descent of the Congo River* by Phil Harwood is a great read for understanding the region.

THE TOWER OF HERCULES
LA CORUÑA, SPAIN

Perched on a windswept promontory on the northern edge of the city of La Coruña, the Tower of Hercules gazes out across the Bay of Biscay, its far-reaching beam of light warning seafarers of the perils of the rocky coast. It is a scene that has played out for 1,900 years since the Romans first landed here and built the lighthouse they called Farum Brigantium. As the oldest lighthouse in the world, the robust Tower of Hercules has become more than a maritime beacon, today standing as a landmark of the city that owes its very roots to the Romans who built it.

The grey stone lighthouse stands on a 57 metre- (187 foot) high rock surrounded by the slapping grey waves of the north Atlantic. It rises a further 55 metres (180 feet) into the sky above the stark, rocky coastline, the higher reaches of the tower restored in the 18th century on top of the original Roman masonry. Through tempests and conquests, invasions and earthquakes the Tower of Hercules has withstood the tests of time. From its vital role aiding ships along the Galician coast during the long Roman period, to its time as a watchtower during the Middle Ages, it has seen the rise and fall of empires. As the star of La Coruña rose in the 15th century, so too did the lighthouse,

the port city sitting on a crucial maritime trading point between northern Europe and the Mediterranean. Its stout, angular form is Neo-Classical in style, the modern electric beacon shining 32 nautical miles out to sea.

Legendary tales have long been told of the tower, handed down through the centuries in folklore. Mythical stories honour the hero Hercules with the founding of La Coruña, the city purported to be built on the grave of the giant tyrant Geryon, slayed by Hercules after a fierce three-day battle. To this day the city's coat-of-arms bears a motif of the tower, a skull and crossbones representing the buried head of Hercules' enemy.

The approach to the lighthouse is as dramatic as its past. A sweeping pathway leads to the entrance, the landscape scattered with statues as part of a 115 acre sculpture park. Inside, 242 steps lead to its highest point, the strenuous hike well worth the effort for the sweeping panoramas over the peninsula, city and out to sea. As the sun begins to set and the great beacon shines its light towards the distant horizon, stand and contemplate the hundreds of people – Romans, Celts and Vikings amongst them – that have stood on that very same spot.

Did You Know?

One of Galicia's most famous dishes is Polbo á feira – octopus pieces sprinkled with paprika. Every year in the mountain town of O Carballiño near Ourense a huge festival takes place in honour of the octopus attended by over 50,000 people.

Take Me There

How to Visit: The Tower of Hercules is located in the city of La Coruña, Galicia. There are flights from Madrid, Barcelona and a handful of international destinations, and plenty of accommodation and tourist opportunities in the city.

Further Information: The official lighthouse website **www.torredeherculesacoruna.com** provides information on visiting and history as does UNESCO **whc.unesco.org**. For details about visiting La Coruña the national **www.spain.info** and regional **www.turismocoruna.com/web** tourism websites are good resources.

EL ALTO/LA PAZ
BOLIVIA

Whichever way you look at it, the mountain metropolis of La Paz and El Alto (technically two different yet overlapping cities) lays claim to its fair share of travel records. At 4,050 metres (13,615 feet) above sea level El Alto, aptly meaning 'The High One', is the highest city in the world. It was once a suburb of La Paz, the world's highest administrative capital city located just a few metres below. Hidden among the seemingly neverending peaks and valleys of the South American Andean ridge, La Paz and El Alto sit within and atop a giant, bowl-like valley where sharp ridges and conical summits meet the altiplano – a vast expanse of mountain plateau desert.

The unfathomably vast and inhospitable moonscape has a harsh and rugged beauty which renders visitors breathless from both the view and extreme altitude. A noisy hubbub roars through the cities' streets, where women waddle down the pavements staggering under the weight of their multi-layered traditional dress, bowler hats balanced precariously atop their heads and a small child slung over their backs.

The lights of El Alto twinkle as the buildings defy gravity, clinging to the sides of a vertical cliff, their smog-blackened facades closing in on the narrow, vertical lanes that radiate outward and upward from La Paz's central main street. Makeshift markets, stalls selling everything and nothing, litter the streets, and balaclava-masked shoe shiners, implying a more sinister profession, grossly outnumber shineable shoes.

Just out of sight of the chaos of the main street is the Witches' Market, a collection of stalls squeezed into tiny, cobbled, colonial-style lanes laden with treasures to fill any cauldron. Dried llama foetuses, frogs and Bolivian armadillos, each with its own healing or protective powers, hang from shop doorways and stalls, creating an eerily mystical ambiance like something from a Harry Potter novel.

While Sucre farther south is Bolivia's official capital La Paz has been the actual centre of government since 1898. Its name translates as 'The Peace,' a bitter irony in a country plagued throughout history by conquest, liberation, poverty and government disputes. Protests and road blockades are part of everyday life, Mardi Gras-style demonstrations marching through the city with regularity. Modern buildings rear their heads between the colonial architecture, a reminder of the city's Spanish roots, and church spires vie for space alongside modern office blocks. It is a delightful combination of old and new, poor and wealthy, classic and modern, two traditional yet developing cities quite literally at the top of the world.

Did You Know?

Connecting La Paz to the Amazon Rainforest is the 35 mile- (56 kilometre) long North Yungas road, a steep, narrow and poorly maintained road flanked by precipitous cliffs. It has been declared the world's most dangerous road and it is estimated up to 300 die every year traversing it. Cycling down it has become one of Bolivia's most popular extreme activities.

Take Me There

How to Visit: International flights from around South America fly to El Alto International Airport from where there is regular public transport to La Paz. There is a variety of accommodation options and bus links to other cities in Bolivia, Peru and Brazil.

Further Information: Guide books to Bolivia can provide detailed travel information. Individual countries' foreign offices will detail possible social conflicts and travel considerations.

AVENIDA 9 DE JULIO
BUENOS AIRES, ARGENTINA

Buenos Aires is a passionate city where the sultry tango is danced from the heart, where red wine and succulent beef are devoured amidst a din of noise, and where the great rivals Boca and River battle it out in front of die-hard football fans. It therefore seems somehow apt that the widest road in the world, Avenida 9 de Julio, should also show off a somewhat flamboyant attitude.

In the heart of vibrant Buenos Aires, Avenida 9 de Julio (Avenue 9th of July) was so named in honour of the country's Independence Day in 1816, and has become an icon of the nation. It is just a mere half mile (approx. one kilometre) in length but spans a full block in width – a precise 110 metres (360 feet) – the city's uniform checkerboard pattern attempting to maintain order amidst the bustle of everyday life. Twelve lanes take what seems an eternity to cross, pedestrians having to wait, foot-tapping and impatient, for several sets of green lights as they march quickly amidst the hungry revving of vehicles.

When the great inter-city thoroughfare was proposed in 1888 it was met with outrage from landlords who ultimately saw their buildings tumble down as the road was carved out – although it took until 1937 until the first phase was completed and a further 30 years until the main section was finished. It was hailed a step towards modernity that would put Buenos Aires on the map alongside the elegant cities of Europe. Indeed, there are echoes of early 21st century Europe everywhere, from the Parisian-esque gardens, statues and fountains that adorn the street, to the bronze statue of Don Quixote. Even the buildings that flank it evoke a certain European flair. The French embassy, which was spared demolition, stands regally and alone, while the magnificent and world-acclaimed Teatro Colón theatre – which has hosted the like of Pavarotti, Maria Callas and Toscanini – is resplendent in Italian marble and French stained glass. And in the centre of the street sits the unmistakable 70 metre- (230 foot) high needle of the Obelisco (obelisk) monument which honours the founding of this spirited, proud metropolis.

Today the street is a living, thrumming part of noisy Buenos Aires. Fervent, flag-toting demonstrators march along its length in their thousands during political protests that pour out of Plaza de Mayo, traffic weaves chaotically from lane to lane, and a deafening roar permeates the air day and night. Stretching from the northern district of Retiro, with its affluent neighbourhoods and shopping avenues, to the crumbling 19th century buildings that surround Constitución Station in the south the street is a true cross-section of Argentinian life.

Did You Know?

Few city squares can attest to the drama of Buenos Aires' Plaza de Mayo. It has seen the beginning of coup d'états, a violent bombing, fervent protests, Eva 'Evita' Peron's rallies of the working classes, and jubilant celebrations led by Maradona for Argentina's World Cup wins.

Take Me There

How to Visit: The road is in the centre of the city and accessible by metro, bus, taxi and on foot.

Further Information: The Official Tourism website **www.argentina.travel/en** and Ministry of Tourism **www.turismo.gov.ar** offer good resources on planning a trip to Argentina. The Buenos Aires tourism website **www.turismo.buenosaires.gob.ar** also offers information on what to see and where to stay (Spanish only).

EAST RENNELL
SOLOMON ISLANDS

Few places in the world are as remote as Rennell Island. Hidden in the far recesses of the Pacific Ocean, 147 miles (236 kilometres) – and an infrequently running twin engine propeller plane ride – away from the Solomon Island's main island of Guadalcanal, it is one of the world's last untouched and undisturbed places. In its eastern part a great ring of cliffs encircles a vast lake 53 miles (86 kilometres) long and 9 miles (15 kilometres) wide, forming the largest raised coral atoll in the world.

Just 1,800 people call Rennell Island home, their Polynesian culture standing them apart from the Melanesian heritage of the almost 1,000 other islands that make up the Solomon Islands. Small villages and their traditional huts dot the shores of the vast Lake Tegano – the largest lake in the Pacific – whose brackish waters teem with tilapia fish, eels and water snakes, and whose abundance of mostly endemic birds have awarded it UNESCO World Heritage status. Rugged limestone islets number in their hundreds, some so small they seem to buckle under the weight of their floppy palm tree inhabitants, and watery caves pocket the shores. The lake is protected by a natural fortress of cliffs that tower 150 metres (492 feet) high, in contrast to the rolling, forested hills of the western part of the island, and a single coral road links the two, down which a handful of rickety vehicles and bicycles trundle in various states of disrepair.

Only the most intrepid of travellers make the journey to Rennell, but those that do find rewards as rich as King Solomon's treasures after whom the islands were named by Spanish explorers. An abundance of wildlife, a strong Polynesian culture and the unique geological phenomenon of the great coral atoll offer genuine back to nature experiences and cultural immersion opportunities few other places can attest to. Try bird-watching in the early morning at 'Motu-manu' (Bird Island), learn to spearfish with local fishermen or bushwalk the rugged paths, spectacular cliffs and sandy, shell-encrusted beaches. By day snorkel the dark corners of the lake in search of the American and Japanese Second World War planes that rest in their watery graves, relics of the great battle of the Pacific, and by night camp under dark skies splashed with stars. Snorkel the clear waters at Tuhugago and Kagaba beaches, keeping an eye out for pods of visiting dolphins, paddle the lake in a dugout canoe or learn basket weaving and traditional fire-making at the handful of eco-lodges scattered around the lake's shores.

Did You Know?

The main language of the Solomon Islands is Melanesian Pidgin, however the islands are home to 120 different indigenous languages. The country has 1,390 kilometres of highways, out of which only 34 kilometres are paved.

Take Me There

How to Visit: There are flights to Rennell from Honiara on the main island of Guadalcanal which receives direct flights from Brisbane, Australia and Port Moresby, Papua New Guinea.

Further Information: The Solomon Island's tourism website www.visitsolomons.com.sb provides detailed travel information and links to eco-lodges and homestays in Rennell. Rennell Island World Heritage Tours organise tailor-made trips and tours.

CEDAR AVENUE OF NIKKŌ
JAPAN

There is a well-known saying in the town of Nikkō, Japan; 'Never say kekko [beautiful] until you see Nikkō'. Nestled within the mountains of Tochigi Prefecture, Nikkō is a city whose sacred past remains ever powerful today. For hundreds of years it has been a centre of Shinto and Buddhist worship, the city a picturesque blend of ornate temples, stunning natural scenery and wild monkeys. Through the heart of it, and running for 23 miles (37 kilometres), is a ceremonial avenue of great cedar trees – the longest tree-lined road in the world.

For almost 400 years Nikkō's cedar trees have lined both sides of the avenue, their great canopies shading temples, shrines and pagodas. They were planted by Matsudaira Masatsuna, a feudal lord serving the Shogun Tokugawa Ieyasu in the 17th century. Following his lord's death in 1616 he constructed the Toshogu Shrine, Nikkō's most famous and elaborate temple, as his final resting place. Leading to the mausoleum he planted 200,000 cedar trees, creating a ceremonial walkway that took 20 years to create and which honours the glories of Japan's Edo period.

Today 13,500 of the trees remain, damage from typhoons and modern-day environmental threats having taken their toll. Yet protective measures are in place to secure their future, and the avenue remains a charming and mystical place. Rocks and stone walls are moistened and protected by the 27 metre- (88 feet) tall trees, blanketing them in an ancient, thick moss and creating an enchanted woodland beneath. From the beauty of a blossoming cherry tree entwined within a cedar, to a civil war cannonball embedded in one of the stout trunks, they tell the stories of Nikkō's past. It is a wonderful experience to wander under the boughs of the building-high trees along the cobbled lane where nature has taken hold.

The cedar avenue is just one of the reasons to visit Nikkō. Multi-coloured temples adorned with gold leaf glimmer in the sun, delicate bridges cross babbling streams and in the distance volcanic peaks rise above the landscape. On the city's doorstep sits the glimmering blue Lake Chūzenji and, at its far end, the Kegon Falls – one of Japan's highest waterfalls – tumbles out of cracks in the mountainside. The seasons change the landscape of the city and its vast National Park; red and gold shines through in autumn, flowers bloom in spring and summer, and in winter steam rises from the numerous hot springs.

Did You Know?

A carving over the door of the Tōshōgū shrine depicts three monkeys in the famous poses of 'see no evil, hear no evil, speak no evil'. The carving is the original source of the now-popular proverb and the Wise Monkeys of Nikkō were the very first in the world.

Take Me There

How to Visit: Nikkō is within easy access of Tokyo by train and is also possible as a day trip. Accommodation options range from budget lodges to traditional guesthouses to luxury hot spring resorts.

Further Information: The official tourism website www.jnto.go.jp offers information on getting to Japan, while for more detailed help on planning a trip to Nikkō visit the Nikkō Tourist Association www.nikko-jp.org/english.

LONGYEARBYEN
NORWAY

It is just 828 miles (1,333 kilometres) to the North Pole and for four months a year darkness shrouds the icy landscape. Docile reindeer amble along the streets, the northern lights dance in a swirl of green and red across the black, starry skies and multi-coloured houses create a dramatic contrast against the blindingly white landscape. Life in the world's northernmost town is unforgiving and harsh, a place where roads are few and far between and snowmobiles outnumber the 2,000 residents two to one. Yet there is an eerie beauty to this remote and inhospitable stretch of Norway's Svalbard archipelago, a frosty and untouched arctic wilderness.

Despite its Norwegian-sounding name, Longyearbyen owes its origins to John Longyear, the American founder of the Arctic Coal Company in 1906. During the Second World War the fledgling mining settlement found itself at the centre of a battle due to its importance as part of the Allied supply chain, and it was ultimately destroyed by German battleships in 1943. Longyearbyen remained unsettled until the end of the war when mining began in earnest once again.

Today in Longyearbyen mining is still the main economy but it also acts as a centre of arctic tourism for the Svalbard region. In winter, snow-mobile and dog-sledding tours head out of the coastal town and traverse glaciers and snow-covered valleys, over wide wintry plains and into frosty caverns decorated with turquoise icicles. It is a time to discover the long heritage of the indigenous Sami people who have herded reindeer for 11,000 years and to attend the Polarjazz festival, the world's northernmost jazz festival.

The summer and winter are like two different worlds in this northerly cluster of islands located mid-way between Norway and the North Pole. After winter's short dark, cold days, summer is the time for hiking and horse-riding over the tundra, fossil-hunting – the world's largest sea carnivore, the Predator X dinosaur, was excavated in Svalbard – and visiting long-abandoned mining settlements like the spooky Russian camp of Pyramiden. To kayak amidst the grandeur of the mighty Isfjorden fjord and watch as its glaciers crack and calve great slabs of ice into the water is a humbling feeling of the power of nature.

Seabirds nest on the cliffs in their thousands during the summer months when the midnight sun basks the land in a golden glow, shy seals poke their whiskered noses above the surface and walruses lounge lazily on chunks of floating sea ice. Polar bears rule the snow-covered mountains and coasts, the world's largest carnivore numbering over 3,000 in the Svalbard islands, more than human inhabitants.

Did You Know?

Longyearbyen is home to the world's northernmost hotel, the Radisson Blu Polar Hotel. The 95 rooms, two restaurants and a sauna were part of the Tråseth Hotel, the American sponsor's hotel during the 1994 Lillehammer Olympics, and the entire wing was moved to Longyearbyen.

Take Me There

How to Visit: There are flights from Oslo and Tromsø to Longyearbyen Airport. The town offers a handful of lodges, guesthouses and hotels and a number of activity providers.

Further Information: Both the Northern Norway Tourism **www.nordnorge.com** and Svalbard Tourism **www.svalbard.net** websites offer a wealth of information on visiting the region. Spitsbergen Travel **www.spitsbergentravel.com** can arrange tours, accommodation and travel packages.

EASTERN STATE PENITENTIARY
PHILADELPHIA

Eastern State Penitentiary struck fear into the hearts of all who laid eyes on its Gothic castle-like exterior. It was an imposing and forbidding stone fortress that was the largest and most expensive building in the United States when it was constructed in 1829. Behind the impenetrable walls, hooded prisoners lived in total isolation, a sentence designed to inspire penitence and true regret. For this was the world's very first penitentiary, a place where physical punishment was abolished, and in its place labour and strict discipline were supposed to create true repentance and spiritual reflection amongst some of America's most notorious criminals.

In 1787 during the age of reform after the American Revolution, a group of powerful Philadelphians gathered in the home of Benjamin Franklin to discuss their concerns with the conditions in American and European prisons, where corporal punishment was an everyday occurrence. They proposed the Quaker-inspired idea of a penitentiary, an idea that would take a further thirty years to become a reality. Its construction shook the world, from its sheer enormity to its architectural design to its radical ideals. Its fame reached the far corners of the planet, and during the early 19th century it became the model on which hundreds of other prisons were built. Long vaulted hallways nine metres- (30 feet) high, towering arched windows and skylights in the cells had echoes of cathedral architecture, and the first seven cells were built around a circular church-like rotunda. Despite its appearance of an enforced monastery, the prison was state-of-the-art, even offering inmates running water, central heating and flush toilets in their cells, luxuries even the White House didn't have at the time.

While the Pennsylvania System of isolation was abandoned in 1913, Eastern State carried on in a different guise, housing increasingly more of the country's worst offenders in shared cells. A dining hall and exercise yard were added, and in 1956 Cellblock Fifteen – Death Row – was the last major addition and the final nail in the coffin of the philosophy that all men could repent. After 142 years of operation Eastern State Penitentiary closed its doors in 1971.

Today Eastern State is an eerie and ghostly shell. Its crumbling walls and empty cells whisper the stories of those who were incarcerated here in total isolation, prisoners such as Al Capone and bank robber Willie Sutton. While art installations and historical exhibits shed light on life behind the walls, from stories of daring escapes to violent riots, exploring the echoing, empty corridors and hollow cells is a chilling and fascinating insight into the world's very first penitentiary.

Did You Know?

Eastern State Penitentiary is considered to be one of the most haunted places in the world and as early as the 1940s convicts reported unexplained visions and spooky experiences. Today over 60 paranormal investigation teams explore the site each year, many for television documentaries.

Take Me There

How to Visit: Eastern State Penitentiary is located in Philadelphia, Pennsylvania and is easily accessible by car or public transport from the city. They offer guided or audio tours.

Further Information: Information on visiting the prison, as well as videos and an online tour are available on the official website **www.easternstate.org**.

DINOSAUR PROVINCIAL PARK
ALBERTA, CANADA

About 75 million years ago the land around modern-day Alberta was lush and subtropical, towering redwoods, palm trees and giant ferns grew in abundance, and amidst this green, fertile paradise dinosaurs roamed in their hundreds. Today those dinosaurs remain, their carcasses buried beneath a landscape of windswept, barren prairie lands, lumps of dry, wrinkled hills, and tufts of hardy grasses. For Dinosaur Provincial Park is the site of the largest discovery of dinosaur skeletons in the world – over 300, with many more yet to be found.

While dinosaurs once roared, scampered and lumbered across the green, fertile terrain, these days it is home to coyotes, Canadian geese and rattlesnakes. Prairie grasslands give way to the lunar-like badlands, where gnarled hoodoo's – towering pillars of fantastically-shaped rock – erupt from the soil, and cacti grow in these northern climes. Through their midst is the great valley of Red Deer River, carved during the last Ice Age, whose banks support cottonwoods and dense sagebrush flats.

Over 23,347 fossils have been unearthed from the prairies, with sharks and amphibians, crocodilians and marsupials amongst them. Yet it is the 40 species of dinosaur discovered here that makes this both a scientific hotbed and fantasy-land of Jurassic Park-like proportions. In actual fact, the dinosaurs that roamed this part of Canada lived during the Cretaceous period, long before the famous Tyrannosaurus and Triceratops. Great lumbering herbivores thrived on the abundant vegetation, from the four tonne Pachyrhinosaurus with its massive flattened head boss, to the fierce-looking, multi-horned Styracosaurus. Duck-billed dinosaurs big and small wandered alongside the fast (and occasionally feathered) two-legged species, and armoured tank-like brutes with spikes along their backs. At the top of the food chain were the carnivores; Daspletosaurus (an early relative of Tyrannosaurus) that stood on two legs three metres (10 feet) tall; the two-tonne Gorgosaurus with its dozens of large, sharp teeth; and small, dog-sized raptors with razor-sharp claws.

Almost 70% of the 31 square miles (81 square kilometre) park is restricted to preserve its paleontological importance, but you can visit as part of a guided excursion. Buses tour the Badlands, you can join an official dig, or embark on a guided hike through the region's stark beauty. Outside of the park, short trails wind through the canyons and gullies, the lush riverside cottonwood forest, and the windswept prairie. Campsites dot the shores of Red Deer River, whose waters just begged to be canoed, and the Tyrrell Museum Field Station in nearby Drumheller is a wonderful addition to a trip to what is the final resting place of the creatures that lived in the 'Age of Reptiles'.

Did You Know?

Drumheller, Alberta is also home to the world's largest dinosaur statue. Made almost completely out of steel it stands 26 metres (86 feet) tall and visitors can climb up into its gaping mouth for panoramic views over the badlands and prairies.

Take Me There

How to Visit: Dinosaur Provincial Park is located 124 miles (200 kilometres) east of Calgary, 30 miles (48 kilometres) north and east of the town of Brooks and accessible from both by public transport. There is a campsite and cabins in the park and others nearby along

Further Information: Detailed visiting information including campsite bookings can be found on the Alberta Parks **www. albertaparks.ca** and Travel Alberta **travelalberta.com** websites.

GLENWOOD HOT SPRINGS
COLORADO, USA

For millions of years hot springs have bubbled from the ground on the banks of the Colorado River. The Ute Native Indians called them Yumpah, their mineral-rich waters and therapeutic tendencies having been tapped long before explorers went in discovery of the legendary springs in 1860. When Walter Horace bought the springs in the 1880s, he opened a vast hot spring pool and lodge on the edge of the dusty fledgling town. As word spread, it rapidly transformed into a world-renowned spa, set within the backdrop of the Rocky Mountains. At 123 metres (405 feet) long and 33.5 metres (110 feet) wide the pool was the largest in the world, a record it still holds almost 120 years later.

Around 16 million litres (3.5 million gallons) of naturally hot mineral water rises from the source of the spring every day. In the frosty winter, when snow blankets the edges of the pool, steam rises from the toasty 34°C (93°F) water into the chilly alpine air. The resort today includes a 107-room lodge and 40°C (104°F) therapy pool, and the original sandstone bathhouse has become the state of the art Spa of the Rockies.

Glenwood Springs was once a rough-around-the-edges frontier town, its position at the confluence of the Colorado River and Roaring Fork River – as well as being on the now historic railroad – quickly bringing it trade, and with it prosperity. As word spread of the hot springs' healing properties, the rich and famous – from film stars to political leaders – arrived from far and wide. Legendary wild west gambler and gunslinger Doc Holliday, infamous for his part in gunfights alongside Wyatt Earp, arrived in search of respite from tuberculosis, the town becoming the setting for both his final months and grave. From outlaws to presidents – President Teddy Rooselvelt spent a summer in the Hotel Colorado – the hot springs have lured people from across the world.

Today the town of Glenwood Springs is both a relaxing retreat and adventure-lovers' paradise, fringed by steep mountains pocked with caves, and lakes wandered by herds of elk. Choose to white water raft the roaring rivers, kayak the lakes, rock climb the precipitous gorges, ski the steep slopes or cycle the mountain trails. And then, when the day is done, slip into the warm, steaming waters of a hot spring pool the length of a football field and let your aches and woes dissolve.

Did You Know?

The Rocky Mountains are home to two famously haunted hotels. In Glenwood Springs' Hotel Colorado guests and staff have reported strange apparitions, smells and noises for decades, while in Estes Park, The Stanley Hotel spooked Stephen King so much it gave him the inspiration for the book *The Shining*.

Take Me There

How to Visit: Denver International Airport is 160 miles (257 kilometres) from Glenwood Springs and there are daily trains to the town's historic station from various destinations in the West and Midwest. Stay at the hot springs lodge, Glenwood Hotel or variety of accommodation options in town. The pool is open daily year-round.

Further Information: Discover more about Glenwood Hot Springs pool, spa and hotel www.hotspringspool.com and www.spaoftherockies.com and travel tips on visiting Glenwood Springs www.visitglenwood.com.

LORD HOWE ISLAND GROUP
AUSTRALIA

Only 400 people are allowed to visit Lord Howe Island at any one time, and the resident population is even less than that. It is just as well too, for this perfect tropical idyll must be Australia's best-kept secret. Just a small blip of volcanic rock a mere 6.8 miles (11 kilometres) long by 1.7 miles (2.8 kilometres) at its widest point, it epitomises everything a paradise island should be; studded with swaying palms, topped with jagged peaks, and adorned with vivid tropical blooms. Empty, pristine beaches are visited by flapping turtles and thick rainforests give way to upland cloud forest. Wrapped around it all is a great swirl of colour teeming with one of the planet's most bountiful marine lives; the world's southernmost coral reef.

In the heart of the Tasman Sea between Australia and New Zealand, the 28 volcanic Lord Howe Islands are considered relative newcomers to the above-water world. Formed seven million years ago, today their land ecology is almost as rich as the vibrant underwater one. Many will be relieved to know that Lord Howe is devoid of the poisonous reptiles, spiders and large sharks that frequent Australia's mainland – although the gentle whale shark does make appearances. Here, bats are the only native land mammal and the indigenous 15 centimetre- (6 inch) long Lord Howe Island stick insect – the largest in the world – thrives on the world's largest volcanic stack. Rising 551 metres (1,808 feet) from the ocean, it is a rocky outcrop known as Ball's Pyramid that lures scuba divers to its maze of trenches, caves and volcanic drop-offs. Below the waves and in the blue skies above is where you'll find most of Lord Howe's faunal residents. Dolphins often escort dive boats on their journeys to the island's 60 dive sites, almost every kind of turtle can be spotted and birds of every size, colour and feather flood the skies.

Lord Howe doesn't have public transport or mobile phone coverage. Its facilities are limited to a handful of family-run shops stocked from the fortnightly boat delivery. Yet those things seem irrelevant in a place where nature most certainly prevails and a sense of tranquillity, peace and charming yesteryear pervades. Visitors come to explore the plentiful reefs, whether by snorkelling in the coral-ringed lagoon or diving in the 30 metre (98 feet) visibility water. They come to hike the lush, forest-covered mountains, to fish for marlin, tuna and giant kingfish, or simply to watch the great migrations of seabirds. For this is a place that seems almost too good to be true, a tangible paradise island that erupted from the depths of the sea.

Did You Know?

The Lord Howe Islands were once a whaling post of the British. When whaling ceased in the late 19th century they turned their hand to the production of the indigenous Kentia palm. The palm is today widely exported and considered the most popular decorative palm in the world.

Take Me There

How to Visit: Lord Howe Island is a two hour flight from Sydney, Brisbane and Port Macquarie. Accommodation ranges from apartments and lodges to the luxury boutique Capella Lodge **lordhowe.com**.

Further Information: For full travel information and advice on planning a trip visit the Lord Howe Island website **www.lordhoweisland.info**. UNESCO **whc.unesco.org** provides further information on the ecology of the region.

BODEGA COLOMÉ
ARGENTINA

High in Argentina's Andes Mountains, the Colomé Winery and Estate manages to blend seamlessly into its surroundings, harnessing the power of the ancestral land through traditional techniques and time-old agricultural methods. Yet it also stands as a complete and delightful contrast. Where the region is rugged and wild, characterised by wrinkled brown slopes, wind-blown alpacas and hardy cacti, the winery is suave and sophisticated. It is a technological feat that has grown from a sparsely inhabited, undeveloped upland region into a world-class winery and state-of-the-art gallery.

Nestled amidst the Upper Calchaquí Valleys at a height of 2,300 to 3,111 metres (7,545 to 10,206 feet) above sea level, the world's highest winery has existed for over 180 years – making it also Argentina's oldest. While its roots might be firmly Argentinian, the current owner is Swiss businessman and wine-maker Donald Hess, who took the reins in 2001 and ambitiously transformed not just the winery but the entire local area. Today, like a green oasis in the middle of the dry and dusty highlands, a beautiful terracotta-tiled, colonial estancia stands at the heart of four estates ringed by snow-capped mountains. To combat the challenges of growing grapes in this arid and isolated environment the very latest technology and equipment has been built, including a full hydroelectric power plant. It is the highest wine-growing region in the world, known as Altura Máxima (Maximum Height). Here the sun shines brighter and with less UV protection, producing thick-skinned grapes strong in health-benefitting antioxidants, resulting in half a million litres of fine wine produced annually and exported to countries across the world. And all of it is organic, biodynamic and cultivated using agroecological practices.

The Malbec wines are refined and complex and the rural boutique hotel elegant and luxurious. Locally-grown vegetables are served on the restaurant veranda from where the views of goats ambling amongst neat vineyards are romantically idyllic. Yet Bodega Colomé has one more surprising trick up its sleeve; a 1,700 square metre (5,577 square feet) exhibition gallery dedicated to the acclaimed modern artist James Turrell. Concerned with light and space, California-born Turrell creates contemporary pieces that mesmerise, startle and cloak visitors in bright lights and colour, and the museum is fantastical and challenging, requiring more energy than the entire bodega to power the installations. In this remote upland landscape ambition and creativity have combined, taking the art of wine to dizzying new heights.

Did You Know?

The Vatican City has the highest per capita wine consumption in the world. The 932 residents of the world's smallest country get through approximately 70 litres (18.5 gallons) per person every year – although it is more likely linked with the wine being sacramental in Catholicism.

Take Me There

How to Visit: There are good connections by plane and bus from Buenos Aires to Salta from where it is necessary to rent a car to reach the winery. It is also possible to use the smaller town of Cafayate to the south as a jumping off point. Reservations are necessary before visiting.

Further Information: The Bodega Colomé website **www.bodegacolome.com** provides information on visiting the winery. For advice on planning a trip to Argentina visit the official tourism authority website **www.argentina.travel**.

MONGOLIA

There is something about Mongolia that can stir emotions in even those who have never stepped foot in the country. It evokes images of huge empty deserts trampled by shaggy, two-humped camels, snow-spattered mountains, vast green steppes and rounded ger tents inhabited by rosy-cheeked herdsmen. It is one of the wildest countries on the planet, a place three times the size of Spain in which paved roads are virtually non-existent outside of the capital Ulanbataar, and where livestock outnumber people 20 to one. For apart from being the world's second largest landlocked country – penned in by Russia and China – it is also the most sparsely inhabited independent country on earth.

There are 2.6 million people living in a wild and unblemished country 603,909 square miles (1,564,116 square kilometres) in size – that works out at around two people per square kilometre. Take into account that almost half of those people live in the capital and it's safe to say there's plenty of room to swing a cashmere goat in the vast tracts of empty wilderness. A third of Mongolians are nomadic, tending their unfenced herds of sheep, goats, cattle, horses and camels in the cold and barren Gobi Desert, the mountains of the north and the green, lake-strewn steppes everywhere in between. They are a people influenced by nature and nomadism, shamanism and Tibetan Buddhism, whose hospitality is as legendary as their wrestling and horse-riding prowess.

Mongolia's past is illustrious and chequered. Since the days when Genghis Khan founded the Mongol Empire it has conquered China and been conquered by China, it has declared independence, come under Soviet rule and revolted against it. Today the country is a peaceful democracy which manages to be both modern and forward-thinking and one of the last few places on earth where a nomadic lifestyle exists.

For travellers, the visiting season is short, the biting winter winds plummeting the mercury to -30°C (–22°F). Summers are hot and for 250 days a year the sun shines in a cloudless blue sky under which Buddhist temples, an abundant wildlife – including the rare snow leopard – dramatic landscapes and rip-roaring festivals await the intrepid. Eco-pursuits abound too, and luxury ger inhabit the wilderness from which you can visit reindeer herders in the High Alpine mountains, explore pristine gorges and lakes, fly-fish in the rivers or ride Mongolian horses. Adventures are open to your imagination in Mongolia – set off on a jeep journey into the deep unknown, plod through the Gobi on a grouchy ship of the desert (camel), race from Europe to Ulaanbaatar as part of the Mongol Rally or hop on the Trans-Siberian all the way to Moscow.

Take Me There

How to Visit: Flights to Ulanbataar connect through Beijing, Seoul or Tokyo, and the Trans-Mongolian section of the Trans-Siberian Railway links the capital with Moscow, Vladivostok and Beijing. There are many ways to explore Mongolia, from independent trips to organised tours.

Further Information: There are many tour operators offering excursions through Mongolia including Nomadic Expeditions **www.nomadicexpeditions.com**. Details of the Mongol Rally can be found at **www.theadventurists.com**.

Did You Know?

There are only two double landlocked countries in the world; Lichtenstein and Uzbekistan. Each of these is fully surrounded by landlocked countries and their residents need to cross at least two borders to reach the sea.

THE ASHMOLEAN MUSEUM
OXFORD, ENGLAND

When, in 1677, prominent antiquary and politician Elias Ashmole presented the University of Oxford with a collection of curiosities he had one stipulation; that they be put on display. Gathered by John Transcendent – Charles I's gardener – on his world travels, the items were varied and eclectic. There were antique coins and books, geological and zoological specimens – including the world's last example of a dodo (long since lost to the ravages of moths). The museum opened on 24th May 1683 and became not only Britain's first public museum, but the world's first to be built for precisely that purpose.

Ashmole's 'cabinet of curiosities' still forms the heart of the modern-day museum. Indeed, the lantern used by the notorious Guy Fawkes during the foiled Gunpowder Plot of 1605 and a sword given by King Henry VIII to the pope are still on display four centuries later. The present museum was formed in 1908 when the Ashmolean and University Art Collection – then housed in the Bodleian Library – were united and moved to the beautiful classical building on Beaumont Street.

A bright, shimmering make-over was revealed to the public in 2009 and has seen the Ashmolean enter a new phase in its long history. Five floors are elegantly packed with antiquities from around the globe – from ancient Greece and China, to prehistoric Europe. Exhibitions depict the great trading routes of Asia, along which merchants, ideas and art united east and west, and a newly opened wing containing some 40,000 Ancient Egyptian and Nubian antiquities, from mummies to a 3,750-year-old funerary boat. There are ancient biblical manuscripts, a death mask of Oliver Cromwell and an impressive collection of treasures from the Catacombs of Rome – indeed, it boasts being the third largest after the Vatican and British Museum. And then there are the paintings, a wonderful display through time and the world from Japan and China to the classic masters of Europe. Discover drawings by Michelangelo, Raphael and Leonardo da Vinci and watercolours by Turner. Paintings bear the unmistakable strokes of Picasso, van Dyck, Cézanne, Constable, Titian, Sargent and many of their compatriots.

Oxford is one of Britain's most famous cities, where traditional punting boats drift up the green-banked river and the elite, world class university has educated politicians, journalists and royals for centuries. Elegant, classical architecture lines the cobbled streets, the university grounds forming the heart of the city centre where, amidst the aura of intellectual promise you will find the oldest museum in the world.

Did You Know?

The dodo bird has become the poster-species for extinction, and its demise can be wholly attributed to man. The last confirmed sighting of the dodo was in 1662 and the largest remains are a head and foot that are on display in the Ashmolean Museum.

Take Me There

How to Visit: The Ashmolean Museum is located in the heart of Oxford, which has extensive public transport links to London and other parts of the UK. There are many sights of interest as well as accommodation and tourist facilities.

Further Information: The Ashmolean Museum website **www.ashmolean.org** has downloadable catalogues and information on current exhibitions. For a comprehensive travel guide to Oxford and Oxfordshire the official tourism website **www.visitoxfordandoxfordshire.com** is an excellent resource.

OMETEPE
NICARAGUA

Ometepe's first native Indian inhabitants believed the ground upon which they stood was sacred. Petroglyphs and stone carvings adorn the island as testament to their passion for the land they called Ome Tepetl – 'the place of two hills'. For the world's tallest lake island is in fact two towering volcanoes, joined together by a low isthmus and forming a great hour-glass 19 miles (31 kilometres) long and three to six miles (five to 10 kilometres) wide.

In the midst of Lake Nicaragua, Ometepe is unmistakable. The twin peaks of Concepción and Maderas point skyward, their lower slopes swathed in jungle and fringed by volcanic black sand beaches. Maderas has long been dormant, its mist-shrouded crater filled with a lake ringed by cloud forest, and fertile slopes blanketed with coffee and tobacco plantations. Capuchin and howler monkeys swing through rainforests teeming with butterflies, birds, wild orchids and ferns, and a cascading 50 metre- (164 foot) high waterfall tumbles through the hidden heart of the nature reserve. On Maderas' quiet and remote slopes small rural villages cultivate the harmonious existence with nature that their Indian ancestors once did, growing organic vegetables in the dark fertile soils, fishing in the great lake, and welcoming visitors to low-key eco-lodges.

At the other end of the island, Concepción is anything but quiet. The perfect, barren cone of the 1,610 metre- (5,282 feet) high volcano looms ominously over the lower slopes, threatening its inhabitants with the possibility of thermal activity. Despite only eight eruptions since 1880 – the latest in 1957 – vapour gases regularly seep out of its summit and occasional lava flows trickle down its angular sides. Ometepe's two largest villages, Moyogalpa and Altagracia, inhabit the lakeside shores of Concepción, their dusty roads traversed by rickety buses, horses and oxen, their wooden churches and rustic buildings flanked by breezy beaches and tropical dry forests.

Ometepe is an eco-paradise, and visitors find they leave cleansed, refreshed and enlightened. With the ever-present volcanoes as a dramatic back drop you can explore the maze of trails where fireflies twinkle beneath plantain trees, take a dip in the clear waters of the lake or kayak the maze of swamps of the Rio Istián, a haven for nesting birds, turtles and caimans. Hike the great peaks and gaze into Concepción's deep crater, or stay in one of the traditional haciendas for a taste of Nicaraguan farm life. There are thermal spring pools and mystical emerald green ponds buried deep in the forests, dramatic sandy beaches engulf the volcanic slopes and a proud cultural heritage is celebrated in more festivals than anywhere else in Nicaragua.

Did You Know?

Lake Nicaragua is one of the few places in the world where there are regular sightings of bull sharks swimming in fresh water, entering the lake by way of the Rio San Juan. The bull shark is one of only two species of shark that can live in freshwater and they are under threat from shark finning industries.

Take Me There

How to Visit: Moyogalpa is the gateway to Ometepe and it can be reached by ferry from San Jorge, Rivas. A new airport also offers flights from Managua. Various low-key accommodations range from backpacker hostels to eco-lodges including Finca Magdalena **www.fincamagdalena.com**.

Further Information: Visit Nicaragua **visitnicaragua.us** offers practical information on visiting the country.

THE GIANT BUDDHA OF LESHAN
SICHUAN, CHINA

With his hands resting gently on his knees and his solemn eyes gazing across the raging confluence of the three rivers that meet below him, the Giant Buddha of Leshan is nothing if not imposing. Standing at a towering 71 metres (233 feet) high this gentle giant's 11 metre- (36 foot) long feet almost touch the swirling river below him and his 15 metre- (49 feet) high head pokes above the hilltop of Xiluo Peak into which he was carved 1,300 years ago.

Here, in the southwest of Sichaun's Chengdu Plain, the towering peaks of the sacred Mount Emei, with its undulating hills, gushing waterfalls and thick pine forests envelope a treasure-trove of Buddhist temples, which make this one of the most important Buddhist sites in China and the world. Ornate ancient stone carvings, shrines, tombs, statues, pagodas and temples are nestled into the natural beauty of the landscape of the Leshan and Mount Emei Scenic Areas, yet none is more remarkable than Dafo (Giant Buddha of Leshan) himself.

Dafo was born from a desperate attempt to calm the turbid waters that plagued the ships travelling down the river. A Chinese monk named Hai Tong believed that the construction of an enormous Maitreya Buddha would ward off the evil water spirits and so began this mammoth feat of ancient engineering. When, in 803, it was finally completed it had taken 90 years to chip and carve out of the hillside – a colossal task at a time when cranes and modern machinery were non-existent. 1,021 perfect buns cover his huge head, his wooden ears are 6.2 metres- (20 feet) long and his shoulders the width of a basketball court.

To truly comprehend the sheer enormity of the Leshan Buddha, stand at his feet – where the sweet smell of incense burns in his honour – and look skywards. It is a humbling feeling. A narrow, dizzying path leads from his head – from where you can gaze into his 3.3 metre- (10.8 foot) wide eyes – down the cliff to the river below. There is an abundance of walking and hiking opportunities in the Leshan and Mount Emei Scenic Areas – together covering 18,000 hectares (44,480 acres) – revealing a magical landscape where the cultural and natural have been woven together, where jagged peaks are home to thousands of species of mammals and birds, and where ancient Buddhist temples have stood for millennia.

Did You Know?

Dafo might be the largest stone Buddha in the world, but he's by no means the largest Buddha. In fact, seven of the top 10 tallest statues in the world are Buddhist depictions – the largest being the Spring Temple, also in China, which measures 153 metres (502 feet), twice the size of the Statue of Liberty. It is soon to be eclipsed however, by the gargantuan, 182 metre- (597 foot) high Statue of Unity – depicting Sardar Vallabhbhai Patel under construction in India.

Did You Know?

How to Visit: Leshan and Mount Emei Scenic Areas are 25 miles (40 kilometres) from one another but together form this significant landscape. Both can be visited from Sichuan's capital Chengdu by public transport or organised tour.

Further Information: Discover more about Leshan and Emei Scenic Areas with UNESCO **whc.unesco.org**. There are many national and international tour agencies offering trips to the region including China Travel Guide **www.travelchinaguide.com**.

MOLOKAI
HAWAII

The sea cliffs of Molokai are breathtaking. Emerald green and forested right up to their boulder-strewn slivers of beach, they stop abruptly as they meet the ocean and plummet into the deep blue sea and crashing waves below. At 800 metres (2,624 feet) high they are the tallest in the world, stretching along a remote coastline on Hawaii's most remote island. Thundering rivers course through the steep valleys and waterfalls crash between the tangle of trees. It is a place of wild, untamed beauty, nature's grandeur at its most dramatic.

Yet in this far-flung corner of Hawaii, where 14 miles (22 kilometres) of majestic pali (cliffs) are battered by the Pacific swells, a small peninsula juts out into the azure seas which belies the peace and tranquillity that today emanates. It is the burial ground of 8,000 Hawaiians, victims of leprosy (today known as Hansen's Disease) who were forcibly quarantined here from 1866. Sufferers of the cruel disease were exiled to this lonely and inaccessible spot, taken from their families to live out their days in segregation – for some the wait was short, for others agonisingly long.

For almost 100 years the Kalaupapa colony existed, long after a cure for the disease was found, and it wasn't until 1969 that Hawaii ended its isolation policy and the few survivors were free to return to civilisation. But the community endures, and a handful of elderly survivors have chosen to live their lives in the oddly quaint little village that is now part of the Kalaupapa National Historical Park. With the rolling cliffs as its backdrop, Kalaupapa is a quiet place of contemplation and a single tour guides visitors around the village where the dead are remembered and survivors honoured. A lone trail descends 488 metres (1,600 feet) down the near perpendicular cliffs where switchbacks weave between forested canyons, a path so narrow it can be traversed only by mule or on foot.

The island of Molokai is a delightful step back in time, a place where palm trees tower over buildings and not a single traffic light exists. It is a rural idyll of long white beaches – the longest in Hawaii – and, at the farthest tip, the fortress of lush green cliffs and cascading waterfalls. Boat and kayak tours provide the best views of the colossal cliffs through waters frequented by humpback whales, and mountaintop lookouts give a sense of the sheer enormity of the rolling peaks from where you can contemplate the irony that one of the darkest times in Hawaii's past unfolded in one of its most beautiful places.

Did You Know?

Of the religious helpers who arrived at the Kalaupapa colony the most notable were Father Damien, who ultimately succumbed to the disease, and Mother Marianne of Syracuse. Both were canonised for their tireless efforts by the Roman Catholic Church.

Take Me There

How to Visit: Father Damien Tours **www.fatherdamientours. com** is the only operator guiding visitors to Kalaupapa and works with Mule Ride **www.muleride.com** for donkey treks and hikes down the cliffs. Ferries and flights operate between Molokai and Maui and there is a wide variety of low-key lodging.

Further Information: Practical travel guides are provided by the Hawaiian national **www.gohawaii.com** and regional **visitmolokai.com** tourism agencies. Further information on the Kalaupapa National Historic Park is provided by the National Park Authority **www.nps.gov/kala**.

XINJIANG
46°17'N 86°40'E, CHINA

To stand on the exact spot furthest from any sea requires an extreme sense of adventure, a good GPS and the following coordinates: 46°17'N 86°40'E. The precise spot – known as the Eurasian or Continental Pole of Inaccessibility (EPIA) – falls within remote north western China, in the upper reaches of Xinjiang Province near the border with Kazakhstan. There is no monument or sign to mark the spot as you would expect for a place of such significance – even the barren, icy realm of the South Pole has a monument (of Lenin). Yet somehow it seems rather fitting that this ultra-landlocked place should be found in a wild and uninhabited part of the world 1,645 miles (2,648 kilometres) from the nearest ocean.

Located in the Dzoonsotoyn Elisen Desert, in a region known as the Dzungarian Basin, the Continental Pole of Inaccessibility is closest to the Arctic Ocean, but not much further from the Bay of Bengal and the Arabian Sea. It is a far-flung, arid and rugged area where the mighty, snow-capped Altai and Tian Shan mountain ranges loom over a great desert basin woven with glacier-fed streams. The western corner is the Dzungarian Gate, a historically important mountain pass that cuts a green steppe through the otherwise impenetrable range between modern-day China and Kazakhstan. These days a highway and railway use the same natural thoroughfare.

To award the title of furthest town from the sea, we need to go no further than 30 miles (48 kilometres) from EPIA to an oasis settlement called Hoxtolgay, a chilly and non-descript place rich in minerals – although the small village of Suluk is just seven miles (11 kilometres) away. The great Silk Road once coursed through these mountains and steppes on its 5,000 miles (8,000 kilometres) journey from Xi'an to Istanbul. Today the modern city of Ürümqi 186 miles (300 kilometres) away is a far cry from the camel caravans of the ancient traders. It was the greatest travel route of all time, along which millions battled the fierce elements and unforgiving geography, from merchants to pilgrims and soldiers to the 13th century traveller Marco Polo.

Today travelling the Silk Road is an epic adventure that will take you close to the EPIA. Either under your own steam by bus or train, or as part of an organised expedition you can follow in ancient footsteps as you cross mountain passes, explore historic cities and, if you can find it, stand at the very centre of the earth.

Did You Know?

The furthest point from land is a spot in the middle of the Pacific Ocean at 48°52.6'S, 123°23.6'W. Known as Point Nemo after the submarine captain in Jules Verne's *Twenty Thousands Leagues Under the Sea*, it can be found in the heart of a piece of water the size of North America, 1,670 miles (2,688 kilometres) from the nearest land.

Take Me There

How to Visit: While China's National Highway 217 and the Kuytun–Beitun Railway both serve Hoxtolgay, Urumqi has an international airport (flights to/from Central Asian countries and cities in China) and good public transport network. There are dozens of tour operators offering Silk Road excursions.

Further Information: Silk Road tours include Intrepid Travel **www.intrepidtravel.com**, Wild Frontiers **www.wildfrontiers.co.uk** and the private trains of Golden Eagle Luxury Trains **www.goldeneagleluxurytrains.com**.

GRAND BAZAAR
ISTANBUL, TURKEY

Istanbul's Grand Bazaar certainly lives up to its name. Around 3,000 shops are spread across 54,653 square meters (13.5 acres) of covered marketplace where up to 400,000 people visit daily to peruse and barter for a myriad of shining, glinting, colourful, scented merchandise sold by thousands of excitable vendors. And all this hustle and bustle, bargaining and touting has been going on for 600 years, making it the world's oldest covered market.

The bazaar is a wonderful maze of labyrinthine streets – 65 of them to be precise – where a chaotic hubbub has rumbled away since 1453 when Mehmet II commissioned it soon after the Ottoman conquest of Istanbul. It started as two small stone bedesten (covered markets) in between which stalls popped up, slowly engulfing the entire Kapali Çarsi neighbourhood. As the empire flourished so too did the bazaar, and by the 17th century it was the heart of Mediterranean trade where textiles, jewellery, spices and weapons were bought and sold. Hans (traveller's inns) appeared around the edge of the marketplace with yet more shops in their courtyards, and mosques, fountains and hammams were built. At night, when the trading was over, 22 gates could be locked shut like a vaulted treasure chest.

The Grand Bazaar has been ravaged by numerous fires and shaken by a violent earthquake over the centuries, yet

has alwa
of its his
a bank,
ferreted
arched
in speci
Fesçiler
Washclo
There w
gold and
hang in
from the

Desp
Grand B
just belo
hookahs
herbs flo
and tiny
and hidd
amidst th
and hage
have don

Did You Know?

The Grand Bazaar was created to fund the Hagia Sofia, a former Greek Orthodox basilica which became an imperial mosque following the Ottoman conquest of Instanbul. It was built in 537AD and was a mosque for almost 500 years when it was secularised and turned into a museum. For 1,000 years it was the world's largest cathedral.

**How to
public tran
city centre

**Further
www.got
trip to Ista
information

USHUAIA
ARGENTINA

In a remote, sub-polar wilderness called *Tierra del Fuego* (Land of Fire) Ushuaia is the very last outpost of civilisation before the great frigid continent of Antarctica stretches to the final ends of the earth. It is a place where the Atlantic and the Pacific meet in a crash of grey, white-capped waves around the infamous Cape Horn, the whipping cold winds and ferocious storms having been the demise of sailors past. Perched on the vast island that was seemingly snapped off the southern tip of South America, the old frontier city of Ushuaia has been many things; at one time a missionary base, a penal colony and, to this very day, the world's southernmost city.

The Andes Mountains end abruptly as they tumble sharply into the sea on this rugged, isolated archipelago separated from the wilds of mainland Patagonia by the Magellan Strait, so named after the great explorer. To the west is Chile, to the east Argentina and the region's capital, Ushuaia, a land of windswept bleakness crammed with jagged, snow-capped peaks and mighty glaciers. The city's jumble of buildings cowers from the elements as they spread down the foot of Cerro Castor (where it is possible to ski 200 metres/656 feet above sea level). Locally-caught king crab is served in the eateries that huddle amidst the wind-battered buildings and the Glaciar Martial blows an icy breath across the city year-round.

Those that venture to this frosty wilderness at the bottom of the world do so in the footsteps of the great explorers whose names are so entwined with its history; Ferdinand Magellan, Charles Darwin, and his captain Fitzroy. Churning at the edge of the city is Beagle's Channel – named after Darwin's ship – a stark and icy 149 miles- (240 kilometres) passageway fringed by glaciers and dotted with rocky isles. Cormorants, sea lions and penguins inhabit the aptly named Bird Island and Seal Island, and Les Eclaireurs Lighthouse attempts to guide seafarers to safety.

Ushuaia's status as capital of Tierra del Fuego has seen the city become the gateway to adventure, where skiing and snowboarding, husky rides and even a frosty golf course, are on the doorstep. Travel the legendary maritime routes by boat, kayak in search of soaring albatross', occasional whales and calving glaciers, or hike the green and forested Tierra del Fuego National Park past lakes and rivers, bays and grasslands. Or set off to explore the very wildest realms of the planet on an Antarctica cruise crossing the turbulent seas of Drake Passage to the white continent.

Did You Know?

The Antarctic ice sheet is 4,776 metres (15,670 feet) deep at its thickest point and averages 2,160 metres (7,086 feet) thick. This comprises 90% of the world's ice and 70% of all the fresh water. There are no land mammals on the 5.4 million square miles (14 million square kilometres) continent.

Take Me There

How to Visit: There are daily flights to Ushuaia's airport from Chile and other parts of Argentina as well as good bus links. Tours can be arranged to the National Park, Glaciar Martial, and other sights. Tours to Patagonia often start or end in Ushuaia and expedition-style and cruise ships depart from here to Antarctica.

Further Information: The official regional tourism website www.tierradelfuego.gov.ar offers useful travel information.

KEUKENHOF
NETHERLANDS

Spring in Holland is a time when the country takes a breath after the long north European winter. The sun shines, the skies are filled with migrating birds and the country's famous tulips are just beginning to sprout their colourful heads above the rich soils. At Keukenhof – the world's largest flower garden – a kaleidoscope of colour bursts through the ground as the park opens its doors for its annual flower show.

The perfectly sculpted gardens are home to over seven million bulbs, where not only the iconic tulip but hyacinths, daffodils, orchids, roses, carnations, irises and lilies sway in the spring breeze, their scents mingling to create a fragrant perfume. Amidst the 32 hectares, 9.3 miles (15 kilometres) of paths weave around exquisite pavilions and statues, and ponds support a variety of butterflies, bees, frogs and swans. The rolling grounds are carpeted with blooming flowers and vivid floral mosaics, each year centred around a different theme, and the nation's florists come to show off their creations in shows and musical flower parades.

For centuries, *Keukenhof* (Dutch for 'kitchen courtyard') was part of the estate of nearby Teylingen Castle, the wooded lands used as hunting grounds for the kitchen of the 15th century Countess of Hainaut. In 1857 the famous landscape architects Jan David Zocher and Louis Paul Zocher – who are attributed with designing Amsterdam's Vondelpark – redesigned the untamed region, bringing the quintessentially English landscape style to Holland. Since 1949 the annual flower show has been one of the country's most spectacular and well-loved events.

Open only for eight weeks a year, the Keukenhof Flower Garden is a mesmerising sight, and there is no better way to feel the advent of spring than by wandering the dainty pathways and soaking in the floral scents in what is known aptly as the 'Garden of Europe'.

Keukenhof sits in the heart of Holland's world-famous tulip farms, ringed by row upon row of tulip fields which disappear into the horizon like great, straight rainbows. There are many opportunities to get lost amidst the blooms, whether it's cycling through the beautiful Dutch countryside, pottering up the canals by electric whisper boat or taking a breath-taking panoramic flight over the endless flower fields.

Did You Know?

When tulips were first introduced to Holland in 1593 they quickly became a highly sought-after luxury of the country's elite. Prices rapidly rose and by the early 1600s even ordinary bulbs were selling for staggering prices – thousands of dollars by today's figures. The economic bubble known as Tulip Mania burst suddenly in 1636 and great fortunes were lost. It is today often regarded as the first ever economic bubble and was one of the most notorious episodes in 17th century Dutch history.

Take Me There

How to Visit: Keukenhof Flower Garden is open from mid-March to mid-May and is located near the town of Lisse, within easy reach from The Hague, Haarlem and Amsterdam. There are dozens of operators offering cycle, boat or plane trips to see the tulip fields from the nearby towns Lisse, Leiden and Den Helder.

Further Information: The Keukenhof website www.keukenhof.nl has a complete list of annual events and practical information and the Holland Tourism Authority www.holland.com provides further information on visiting the tulip fields.

HAIFA
ISRAEL

At 1.1 miles (1.8 kilometres) long it would be logical to assume that walking between stops would be faster than using Haifa's mini metro. Yet take one look at the topography and it becomes clear why it was such a well-received addition to this pretty, laid-back Israeli city. Tumbling down the northern slopes of the Carmel Mountain ridge on the Mediterranean coast, Haifa is so steep that the metro line is more like an underground cable car (incidentally, there is also one of those in Haifa). Built in the 1950s, shortly after the creation of the State of Israel, the Carmelit Subway was at the time in the heart of the city centre, linking together its historic neighbourhoods otherwise joined by hundreds of heart-pumping, higgledy-piggeldy steps. Today Haifa is a cosmopolitan, expanded city that stretches to the golden sandy beaches in the south, the modern port and cruise ship terminal in the north and the university perched high on the tip of Mount Carmel. Six stops deposit passengers in Haifa's decoupage of charismatic neighbourhoods, each emanating its very own traditions, architecture and ambience.

Crusaders and Carmelites, German Templars and Bahá'í have made their indelible marks on Haifa during its long history. Dominating the skyline is the city's most iconic sight, the immense golden dome of the Shrine of Bab and immaculately manicured Persian gardens. It is the world centre and one of the holiest sites of pilgrimage for members of the Bahá'í faith, built in 1953 over the burial place of the Bahá'í founder. At its foot is the German Colony – built by the Templars in 1969 – where a wide boulevard is lined with white stone houses, pretty courtyards, trendy café's and leafy trees. From the Wadi Nisnas souk (market) with its traditional Arabic eateries, to the central Carmel neighbourhood, with its upmarket hotels and sea views, the Carmelit Metro links them all.

Israel's third largest city doesn't profess to have the historical intrigue of Jerusalem nor the flamboyance of Tel Aviv, but is happy to revel in its own unique charm. World class museums abound, it has a rich history, where the 12th century Carmelite monastery was once used as a hospital for Napoleon's failing army, and the cave in which Elijah the Prophet is believed, according to tradition, to have spent many years living in and which is worshipped by Jews, Christians, Druze and Muslims. Haifa's metro might be small but its history is long and its appeal enormous.

Did You Know?

The Bahá'í religion is the youngest of the world's independent religions and is considered one of the fastest-growing and most widespread. There are currently more than five million Bahá'ís living in 100,000 localities throughout the world. The scriptures have been translated into over 800 languages.

Take Me There

How to Visit: Israel is served by the Tel Aviv International Airport from where there are good public transport links to Haifa. The Carmelit Railway is open Sunday to Friday midday, and the city has many excellent tourist facilities.

Further Information: Information on tickets, stations and running times can be found on **www.carmelithaifa.com**. For travel tips on visiting Haifa and Israel the local **www.visit-haifa.org** and national **www.goisrael.com** tourism authorities offer good guides.

VICTORIA FALLS
ZAMBIA/ZIMBABWE

Victoria Falls isn't the highest waterfall in the world – that accolade goes to Venezuela's Angel Falls. It isn't the widest either, being ever so slightly topped by South America's Iguazu Falls. But it is the largest – a staggering 1,708 metres (5,604 feet) wide and 108 metres (354 feet) high which forms the world's greatest sheet of falling water. Its indigenous name is *Mosi-oa-Tunya*, 'The Smoke That Thunders', for the mighty Zambezi River roars over a flat plateau and disappears into a chasm-like open mouthed gorge creating a cloud of mist so high it can be seen over 18 miles (30 kilometres) away.

The Zambezi River and Victoria Falls form a natural border between Zambia and Zimbabwe, the river flowing gracefully over a flat plateau flanked by national parks teeming with African wildlife. Tree-covered islands sit in its midst right up to the precipitous point where it collapses over the lip of the gorge. Two islands exist on the edge of the falls, the larger – Livingstone Island – named for David Livingstone, the Scottish explorer and first European to set eyes on the cascades in 1855. Today, nerves-of-steel visitors bathe in the 'Armchair' or 'Devil's Pool' on the island, just a few metres from where the water crashes over the falls.

There are two sides to Victoria Falls, not just politically but metaphorically too. On the one hand it is staggeringly beautiful and visitors arrive to gawp in wide-eyed amazement at the sublime beauty of Mother Nature. When the river is in full flood 540 million cubic metres of water fall over the edge every minute, creating a mist that plumes 400 metres (1,312 feet) in the air and rains life on the forests on its shores. Sunny rainbows and ethereal moonbows glow in the spray and hippopotamuses, crocodiles and elephants are riverside visitors. On the other hand it is an adventure junkie's paradise, the wild ferocity of the falls creating an adrenaline rush that can only be satiated by bungee jumping off Victoria Falls Bridge, white water rafting the torrents or zip-lining across Batoka Gorge.

Towns on both sides of the river – Maramba in Zambia and Victoria Falls in Zimbabwe – offer access to the falls, where names such as Knife-Edge Bridge and the Boiling Pot speak for themselves. You can take to the air in a helicopter for a swooping bird's eye view or cruise in a jet boat for a wet close-up. There are bush walks and elephant safaris, horse-riding in the forest or fly-fishing on the Zambezi, mountain-biking the gorge's cliffs and genteel river safaris.

Did You Know?

In nearby Botswana is the vast Chobe National Park which is home to the Kalahari elephants – the largest species in the world. Enormous herds wander the savannahs in what is believed to be the highest concentration of elephants on the planet.

Take Me There

How to Visit: Victoria Falls can be visited from Victoria Falls town (Zimbabwe) or Maramba (Zambia) and both are accessible by road, rail and air. There are numerous resorts and hotels in the towns and campsites in the national parks.

Further Information: Both the Zambia www.zambiatourism.com and Zimbabwe www.zimbabwetourism.net tourism websites offer comprehensive guides to visiting the falls. Another good resource is the Zimbabwe Parks and Wildlife Management Authority website www.zimparks.org.

THE VIA APPIA ANTICA
ROME, ITALY

In Italy's busy capital a stream of buses, cars and scooters chug along one of the many paved roads and hundreds of feet pound the cobbles. At first glance the road is unremarkable, just another in a city strewn with ancient relics of grand proportion. Yet this is a road that has seen the dawn of centuries, the greatest highway in the Roman Empire which stretched as straight as the horizon into which it disappears all the way to the port city of Brindisi on Italy's eastern coast.

Strategically the Via Appia Antica was Rome's first and most crucial thoroughfare, forming a gateway to the East along which soldiers and traders marched. In its entirety it covered 350 miles (563 kilometres), a great artery along which rows of sandal-shod Roman soldiers paraded and which passed goods that set sail to Egypt and Greece.

Rome's poignant and powerful past can be seen in the relics that line the road. Great, elaborate tombs stand on either side of the roadway, the final resting place of the city's elite. Amongst the tombs of emperors and philosophers the most impressive is that of Cecilia Metella, the wife of one of Julius Caesar's generals. It was also along the Via Appia where it is believed St Peter had a vision of Jesus as he fled persecution in Rome, and today the simple Baroque church of Chiesa del Domine Quo Vadis stands as testament.

Death was very much part of the life of the Via Appia Antica. The bodies of 6,000 crucified slaves were strewn along it for miles in 73BC after their revolt proved no match for a fierce Roman army led by the mighty Spartacus. Beneath the great basalt slabs lay the bodies of early Christians, popes and martyrs buried in a maze of tunnels and catacombs.

Today the ancient road is woven into the city that bustles around it. The first 10 miles (16 kilometres) fall within the specially designated Appia Antica Park which, outside of the busy traffic areas, is a fascinating place to walk or cycle. Tours lead visitors into the gloomy underground of the Christian catacombs or on open-top buses from where it is possible to spy the crumbling temples and churches that flank it. On Sundays, when the park closes to private vehicles, wander along the stone slabs and reflect on those who have walked before you as the phrase 'I am Spartacus' teeters on your lips.

Did You Know?

The Via Appia might be the oldest road still in use today but there are many ancient roads far older. The oldest paved road in the world is in Giza, Egypt – built 4,600 years ago – and was used for transporting the basalt to build the great pyramids.

Take Me There

How to Visit: Sections of the Via Appia can be visited on foot, by bicycle, by public bus or by tour bus. The Appia Antica Park is easy to visit from central Rome and the tourist information centre has maps and bicycle rental.

Further Information: The Appia Antica Park website www.parcoappiaantica.it provides information on visiting the area. Bus tours are arranged by Trambus Open www.trambusopen.com and tours to the catacombs through www.catacombe.roma.it. For information on visiting Rome the city tourism website www.turismoroma.it is a good resource.

YELLOWSTONE NATIONAL PARK
USA

Around 640,000 years ago a volcano erupted with enough ferocity to form a crater 34 miles (55 kilometres) by 35 miles (56 kilometres). In it mud boiled, vapours hissed from the ground in tall plumes and steam rose from the rivers that coursed through. That land is Yellowstone, a place where half the geothermal features and two thirds of all the geysers in the world are concentrated in a fantastical wonderland of fumaroles, psychedelic-coloured thermal pools and gurgling hot springs. With the huge caldera at its heart the region was declared a national park in 1872 – the very first in the world.

Yellowstone hasn't much changed since the days when the first white man, John Colter, stepped foot in a land mockingly called 'Colter's Hell' by those who disbelieved his accounts of a place of fire and brimstone. Herds of shaggy bison still roam the sprawling grasslands in their thousands and steam spurts from holes in the earth's crust. It is a captivating landscape of bizarre geothermal activity, perfect alpine mountain ranges, roaring rivers, tumbling waterfalls, and ancestral wildlife. While Native American Indians no longer hunt these lands, great herds of elk graze amidst the thick pine forests, bighorn sheep clamber on rocky precipices and bears – grizzlies and black – amble through wildflower meadows. The most abundant wildlife in the lower 48 states thrives here, in a place that despite being visited by three million people a year remains a true wilderness of grey wolves, coyotes, badgers, red foxes, bobcats, raccoons, moose, beavers, otters, bald eagles and mule deer.

Located in the highlands of Wyoming amidst the formidable Rocky Mountains, Yellowstone seems to do everything on a grand scale. It measures a staggering 3,468 square miles (8,983 square kilometres), and water pours through the 24 mile- (38 kilometre) long pink and yellow walls of the Grand Canyon where the Lower Falls cascade from 94 metres (308 feet) high. Geysers spout steaming fountains 55 metres (180 feet) into the air with the clockwork regularity of Old Faithful or the elusive unpredictability of Steamboat – the world's tallest.

Yellowstone isn't the kind of place you can visit in a day. It is a place to savour and explore, a place where you should both venture off the beaten path and photograph the iconic sights. There are 1,100 miles (1,800 kilometres) of trails to be hiked in summer or skied in winter, stars to be camped under and streams to be fished. Kayak past lakeside geysers, horse-ride through herds of ambling bison and discover the park's long history from its Native American heritage to its dinosaurs and gold mining.

Did You Know?

Many towns in Yellowstone country have a rodeo and it is an important part of the region's cultural heritage. Every July in Cheyenne, Wyoming over 200,000 people attend the Cheyenne Frontier Days rodeo – the largest in the world.

Take Me There

How to Visit: There are domestic airports in Cody, Jackson and Idaho Falls and the international airports in Salt Lake City and Denver. There is no public transport within the park but tour companies offer trips. There is a variety of accommodation options both inside the park and within the surrounding valley.

Further Information: The National Parks Service **www.nps.gov** offers a comprehensive visitor's guide, and there is a wealth of information on **www.yellowstonepark.com**. Discover more about Cheyenne Frontier Days at **www.cfdrodeo.com**.

LÆRDAL TUNNEL
NORWAY

When the King of Norway cut the ribbon to open the Lærdal Tunnel in November 2000 he did so to great celebration. For two ancient communities were finally joined. An arduous journey that once traversed the high mountain passes in summer and the deep fjords in winter – when the so-called Snow Road was unpassable – could now be accomplished in just 20 minutes. The tunnel is the longest ever constructed, 15.2 miles (24.5 kilometres) of road carved out of the belly of the 1,809 metre- (5935 foot) tall mountains that formed a formidable barrier above it.

It's not surprising that the world's longest tunnel is here, at the northern end of Norway's longest fjord. Forested cliffs, huge snow-covered peaks and ice-cold waterfalls create one of the most breathtaking landscapes on the planet, but one that for centuries has put all who live here at its mercy. The tunnel was a dramatic and challenging feat of engineering. It cost the Norwegian government $13 million US dollars, with 2.5 million cubic metres (3 million cubic yards) of rock being carved out to make way for the two-lane road. The tunnel is so long that the mental strain on drivers and the effects of claustrophobia are serious threats. Rest stops are frequent and these mountain caverns are lit by blue lights fringed with yellow to give the impression of a calming sunrise. Buried deep beneath ground a huge cavern houses an air treatment plant – the first such one in the world – ensuring the air remains clean and fresh.

Thanks to the tunnel, the important route between Oslo and Bergen is now ferry-free and independent of the seasons. It has also opened up the Sognefjord region, a place of wild nature, staggering views and historic villages. Kayaks glide along the dark, mirror-flat water past farms, grasshopper green fields and thundering waterfalls, and hikers climb through lush pastures and up forested slopes for top-of-the-world views.

At the northern end of the tunnel is Lærdal, a picturesque town of historic wooden houses, ancient churches and a river teeming with salmon. Farming is the cornerstone of life here and visitors can try their hand at deer herding or baking bread in the traditional stone ovens. A quick drive through the tunnel emerges in Aurland, a province of enormous natural features dotted with tiny villages. It is one of the best regions for getting to one with Norway's nature and historic traditions; take the steep, scenic train from the beautiful village of Flåm; explore the Viking village in Gudvangen; or go in search of wildlife on a fjord safari.

Did You Know?

The Flåm Railway is one of the steepest railways in the world. At a stomach-lurching gradient of 55% it snakes through 20 tunnels on its 12 mile (19 kilometre) journey through the region's wild scenery.

Take Me There

How to Visit: The tunnel is a five-hour drive from Norway's capital, Oslo and links the municipalities of Aurland and Lærdal. The village of Flåm is located in Aurland a few minutes' drive from the entrance to the tunnel. There is a multitude of accommodation options including romantic guesthouses and charming hotels.

Further Information: The national www.visitnorway.com and regional www.sognefjord.no; www.visitflam.com tourism websites provide lots of excellent information on visiting the region including accommodation options.

THE PANTANAL
BRAZIL

As the sun begins to set a jeep trundles and bounces its way along the dirt track through overhanging foliage. Startled birds shoot out of the undergrowth crowing their surprise; heavy-beaked toucans flapping furiously, rare blue hyacinth macaws and vivid green parrots. As dusk descends a trail of glowing fireflies is left in the wake, Caiman alligators lounge lazily in the evening warmth and Labrador-sized capybara, the world's largest rodent, amble back to their dens.

The Pantanal, located in Brazil's southwest (and drifting into Bolivia and Paraguay), is a vast and savage wetland, the largest on the planet and over 10 times the size of Florida's Everglades. An enormous landlocked river delta, its waters rise and fall with the seasons creating one of the most biologically rich environments in the world. In contrast to the Amazon Rainforest, where birds, animals and reptiles remain elusive in the dense jungle, the Pantanal's open wetlands, rivers and marshes make it one of the planet's best wildlife-spotting regions, a perfect and abundant circle of life second only to Africa's teeming reserves.

Sporadic cattle ranches inhabit the few raised areas of land offering rustic and authentic accommodation for hardy visitors. Horses are the main mode of transport, their hooves specially adapted to wading through pools adorned with great lily pads and ambling past sunbathing anacondas wrapped powerfully around tree branches. Hundreds of eyes belonging to Caiman alligators pop above the surface of the water, Capuchin and Howler monkeys swing through the tree tops, tapirs can be spotted in the watery fields, peccaries (wild pigs) grunt and splash through the swamps and giant otters ply the rivers in search of their favourite food, red-bellied piranhas. It is a swirl of colour and life, an ecological honey-pot filled with butterflies, insects, blossoming flowers, schools of fish and birds of every size with feathers of every colour.

Life in the Pantanal is at the mercy of the seasons. The wet season from October to March, makes travel difficult, while the dry season, from April to September, provides some of the best chances of spotting South America's most famous resident, the jaguar. Low-key eco-tourism offers adventurous travellers the chance to stay in the heart of one of the world's great natural wonders, where horse-riding, fishing, boat trips and wading are super-sized adventures in a land where even the mosquitoes are the size of flies and the 1.5 metre- (5 foot) tall Jabiru stork doesn't even come close to being the largest bird.

Did You Know?

Ex-US President Theodore Roosevelt embarked on a dangerous scientific expedition into the heart of the Pantanal in 1913–14 with Brazilian explorer Cândido Rondo. Despite great hardships, during which Roosevelt almost died, they were the first non-native explorers of the 1000 miles (1,610 kilometres) long River of Doubt whose name was later changed to Rio Roosevelt in his honour.

Take Me There

How to Visit: The Pantanal is served by Cuiabá and Campo Grande airports, which connect to São Paulo. Light aircraft or jeep tours take visitors to the cattle stations for two- to six-day trips from both cities as well as Corumbá or Miranda.

Further Information: UNESCO whc.unesco.org provides information on the region's ecology. There are many good tour companies including Pantanal Nature Wildlife Tours www.pantanalnature.com.br and Pantanal Explorer pantanalexplorer.com.br.

GRAND CANAL
CHINA

Few haven't heard of China's most famous ancient monument, the Great Wall. The world's longest wall and longest military structure snakes 5,500 miles (8,850 kilometres) from east to west following the southern edge of Inner Mongolia, and once defended the country from Mongol and Manchu attacks. Yet the Great Wall isn't the only Chinese man made structure to carve its way through the country, breaking records with every twist and turn. At 1,104 miles (1,776 kilometres) long, the Grand Canal is the world's longest artificial waterway, stretching from Beijing in the north to Zhejiang province in the far south, the ancient artery having flowed for over 1,200 years.

During the Sui Dynasty, the industrious Emperor Yang came up with an idea, one which would change the face of China for centuries to come. In order to overcome the hurdle of China's east to west-flowing rivers, he commissioned a vast and ambitious river be built stretching from Beijing and connecting to the Yangtze River in the south. It was a huge feat of engineering, built by over a million farmers, which fused the vastly different and largely unconnected northern and southern regions of the country and became the backbone of the Empire's transportation system. For 14 centuries barges have chugged up and down the canal carrying rice and grain from the fertile paddies around the Yangtze River Delta to the political powerhouse cities. Yet it did far more than shuttle soldiers and food, it became the thoroughfare along which cultural traditions and ideas sailed.

These days the canal remains an important highway, although great tracts hold little appeal, weaving between industrial, modern cities and along mile after mile of agricultural land. Yet there are still places where time has stood still for the Grand Canal, where life on the river's edge continues as it has done for centuries. In the towns and old cities of Jiangsu and Zhejiang provinces, small cruise boats vie for space amongst the small, rustic barges that hurtle along the muddy brown waters. They pass ancient crumbling riverside houses, squeezed together in a disorganised jumble, slip under arched stone bridges from which dangle red Chinese lanterns, and sail past fishermen and their trusty cormorants. The canal has been the lifeblood of China since long before the automotive was invented and to this day remains a pumping artery along which great coal ships sail and historic towns defend their traditional way of life.

Did You Know?

The belief that you can see the Great Wall of China from the moon (or space) is actually a very old myth. Seeing the wall with the naked eye from the moon would be the equivalent of seeing a human hair from two miles (3.2 kilometres) away.

Take Me There

How to Visit: The best places to experience ancient canal life are in the cities of Suzhou, Hangzhou, Huai'an and Wuxi from where it is easy to arrange a day cruise. There is also a Grand Canal Museum in Beijing.

Further Information: As a designated world heritage site there is more information on the Grand Canal on the UNESCO website **whc.unesco.org**. Travel tips on visiting China are provided by the national tourism office **www.tourismchina.org**.

THE 'FALKIRK TRIANGLE'
SCOTLAND

It all started in 1989 when, in the very ordinary little town of Bonnybridge, Scotland, witnesses reported seeing a hive of inexplicable night time activity. They described red and white objects whizzing in the skies, then racing towards them as close as six metres (20 feet) away, before veering off and disappearing. As unidentified flying objects they were, by definition, UFO's and by no means the last strange sightings reported in the town. Throughout the 1990s the area between Bonnybridge, Falkirk and Stirling – dubbed the 'Falkirk Triangle' – was the scene of hundreds of reports of strange goings-on. To this day there are over 300 reported annual UFO sightings, the most anywhere on planet earth.

Why, should the sightings ever conclusively be proven to be aliens, they would choose the Falkirk Triangle over anywhere else might just be the bigger mystery. It does hold a certain tourist charm, that's undeniable. It's a stone's throw from the most complete surviving Roman fort along the Antonine Wall. The legendary William Wallace battled in these parts and there is an impressive monument to him in Stirling. Beautiful Loch Lomond beckons enticingly in The Trossachs National Park, and there are more castles than you can shake a haggis at. If extra-terrestrials are in search of a bit of Scottish history and natural beauty then they've come to the right place but, despite repeated calls for an investigation into the strange sightings by the mayor of the town, the UFO's still remain precisely that.

Residents and visitors have reported bright pulsating lights forming moving shapes in the sky. Some have chased cars. Lights the size of houses have been seen landing in fields, and some witnesses tell of being pursued. Through the 90s the stories came thick and fast, threatening to push the Loch Ness Monster off her throne as most unexplained Scottish mystery. Yet with the advent of modern technology, many of the unusual happenings have been caught on camera – one resident has over 18 hours of video which, when reviewed by the Search for Extraterrestrial Intelligence Institute in the United States came back as 95% UFO.

Sceptics explain the activity as secret military testing from Scotland's numerous bases. Others say it's all a ruse to garner media and tourist attention. Yet none of it has done anything to stop the region from becoming the top spot on the extra-terrestrial hunting map. For every theory there are sceptics to counter-argue. Perhaps, if it is aliens above the skies of Scotland, they will come and introduce themselves one day. Until then, they remain just out of reach.

Did You Know?

In 1947, a flying object crashed on the outskirts of Roswell, New Mexico. Although the US government explained it as a surveillance balloon, conspiracy theories have been rife since the 1970s and Roswell has become the most famous possible UFO landing in history. There is even a flamboyant annual festival in the town **www.ufofestivalroswell.com**.

Take Me There

How to Visit: The 'Falkirk Triangle' is easily accessible from Glasgow and Edinburgh, and there are tourist facilities throughout the region.

Further Information: Visit Scotland **www.visitscotland.com** has an excellent guide to the country, including activities in the Falkirk region. To learn more about UFO sightings the Search for Extraterrestrial Intelligence Institute **www.seti.org** is a good resource.

KWAZULU NATAL COAST
SOUTH AFRICA

Come May along South Africa's KwaZulu Natal coast, a sense of anticipation hangs in the air and sea. Locals, tourists, birds and ocean predators gather to wait in breath-held suspense for one of the planet's most spectacular shows to commence: the great sardine run. Billions of sardines – technically they're Southern African pilchards – head north along the cold currents all the way to Mozambique and then veer off into the Indian Ocean It is a great dark mass just under the surface of the sea often measuring 4.3 miles (7 kilometres) long, 0.9 miles (1.5 kilometres) wide and 30 metres (98 feet) deep.

Like a huge writhing animal the sardines swim together, counting on safety in numbers to protect them from the entourage of predators that trail the run along the coast. It is an all-out feeding frenzy, the silvery fish attacked in an aerial assault by swooping Cape Gannets, cormorants, terns and gulls, and from the cold depths by South Africa's biggest hunters. Common and bottlenose dolphins – numbering some 18,000 – expertly round their prey into tightly packed bait balls 10 to 20 metres (33 to 65 feet) in size before darting through to gorge on the sardines.

Sharks, mainly Bronze Whalers, but also Dusky, Grey Nurse, Blacktip, Hammerheads, Great Whites and Zambezi sharks gorge themselves on the plentiful food, and game fish from Bluefish to King Mackerel get in on the action. Cape Fur Seals follow the shoals from their spawning grounds on South Africa's Cape as far as Port St Johns, and Bryde's whales can be seen breaching in the choppy waters.

Why the sardines makes this long and arduous journey remains a mystery. In some rare years they simply don't make an appearance, perhaps migrating in deeper, colder waters or just not at all. Like the great wildebeest migrations for which Africa is so famous, the sardine run is one of the world's greatest wildlife spectacles – some experts believe the biomass could indeed exceed the wildebeest – and people descend on the coast to witness it for themselves. Light aircraft buzz in the skies keeping a lookout for the silvery bands of sardines, and dive boats offer you the opportunities to watch from the deck, don a snorkel and drift in the cold ocean currents or delve beneath the waves for a heart-pumping scuba dive amidst one of the planet's grandest wildlife phenomena.

Did You Know?

South Africa's waters are popular feeding grounds of Great White Sharks, the largest predatory fish on the planet. The powerful animals grow to an average 4.6 metres (15 feet) long, but sharks measuring up to six metres (20 feet) and weighing 2,268 kilograms (5,000 pounds) are not unheard of.

Take Me There

How to Visit: For those arriving in South Africa just to see the sardine run then Durban Airport is the closest port of entry and connects to Johannesburg International Airport. From May to July week-long excursions are run by dive operators all along the coast but get booked up well in advance.

Further Information: The official South African tourism authority website **www.southafrica.net** is a good first resource for planning a trip to the country. There are many outfits offering sardine run excursions including Seal Expeditions **www.sardinerun.com**. Apex Predators **www.apexpredators.com** and African Dive Adventures **www.afridive.com**.

PHOTO CREDITS

1 Hang Son Doong Cave © Ryan Deboodt

2 Millau Viaduct © Eiffage CEVM/ Foster&partners/D.Jamme

3 Salar De Uyuni © Guido Amrein, Switzerland SS; © abc7 | SS

4 309 AMARG © 309 AMARG; © John Saunders

5 Sermeq Kujalleq © Rino Rasmussen

6 Chernobyl and Pripyat T © Oliver Sved | SS; BR © Liukov | SS; BL © BPTU | SS

7 Mount Thor © Grant Dixon; © Parks Canada

8 USS Oriskany © Amar and Isabelle Guillen - Guillen Photo LLC / Alamy

9 The Dead Sea © vvvita | SS; © Nickolay Vinokurov | SS

10 Bishop Rock © Pictureperfect79 | DT; © Andrew Roland | SS

11 The Namib Desert T © Marisa Estivill | SS; BL © Eric70 | SS; BR © mezzotint | SS; © Galyna Andrushko | SS

12 Ilha Grande © Diego Cardini | SS

13 Tristan Da Cunha © Alexey German-Oceanwide Expeditions

14 Smithsonian Institution © National Air and Space Museum, Smithsonian Institution.

15 Ngorongoro Crater © Pal Teravagimov | SS; © Tr3gi | DT

16 Monaco © ostill | SS

17 Mount Stromboli © luigi nifosi | SS

18 Great Mosque of Djenné © Quick Shot | SS

19 Daintree © Ralph Loesche | SS; © Wagsy | SS

20 The American Queen © American Queen Steamboat Company

21 Dallol © Matej Hudovernik | SS

22 San Alfonso del Mar © Crystal Lagoons

23 Maldives © R McIntyre | SS; © Galyna Andrushko | SS

24 MUSA Cancun © Jason deCaires Taylor

25 Angel Falls © Alice Nerr | SS

26 Westray © Dieter Lion | DT

27 Lake Baikal © Mikhail Markovskiy | SS; © Golden Eagle Luxury Trains

28 Hassan II Mosque © Mikadun | SS

29 Cherrapunji & Mawsynram © Daniel J. Rao | SS

30 Lalibela © Anton_Ivanov | SS

31 Cotahuasi © Rafal Cichawa | SS

32 Ironbridge © tomfoxall | SS

33 The Empty Quarter © David Steele|SS

34 San Pedro Sula © Charles Harker|SS; © soft_light | SS

35 Great Blue Hole © Tami Freed | SS

36 Bucharest Palace of Parliament © Anton_Ivanov | SS; © Aleksandar Todorovic | SS

37 Crater Lake © saiko3p | SS

38 Highway 1 Australia © Markus Gann | SS

39 Moyenne Island © Purestock | Thinkstock

40 Abu Simbel © Waj | SS

41 Mosquito Bay © Puerto Rico Tourism Company

42 Eden Project © Francesco Carucci | SS

43 Mount Chimborazo © ache1978 | SS

44 ICEHOTEL Dragon Residence - Artists: Dorjsuren Lkhagvadorj & Bazarsad Bayarsaikhan © Paulina Holmgren

45 Puerto Princesa © r.nagy | SS; © saiko3p | SS

46 Borobudur © Pigprox | SS

47 Kvarken Archipelago © TTphoto | SS

48 The Canton Tower © feiyuezhangjie|SS

49 Fraser Island © electra | SS; col | SS

50 El Sobrino de Botín © Restaurante Botin

51 Lake Titicaca © Steve Allen | DT; © Rafal Cichawa | SS

52 Schönbrunn Zoo © Jeff Whyte | SS; © Mariia Golovianko | SS

53 General Sherman © Alexander Petrenko | SS

54 Kolukkumalai © Pikoso.kz | SS

55 Lake Turkana © Piotr Gatlik | SS

56 Burj Khalifa L © Sophie James | SS;

R © Anna Omelchenko | SS

57 The Sundarbans © neelsky | SS

58 Sublimotion © Sublimotion

59 Atacama Desert © Guido Amrien | DT; © Nataliya Hora | SS

60 Ulm Minster © Mikhail Markovskiy | SS

61 Oymyakon © Bolot Bochkarev

62 Tyne Cot Cemetery © chrisdorney|SS

63 Frying Pan Lake © Waimangu Volcanic Valley; © Filip Fuxa | SS

64 Potala Palace © qian | SS

65 Cox's Bazar © Mohammad Moniruzzaman

66 Qinghai-Tibet Railway © Jun Mu | SS

67 Ngerulmud © Fish n Fins Palau; © optionm | SS

68 King Fahd Fountain © urosr | SS

69 The Congo River © Ferdinand Reus | DT

70 Tower of Hercules © Anibal Trejo | SS

71 El Alto/La Paz © Christian Kohler | SS; © Galyna Andrushko | SS

72 Avenida 9 de Julio © meunierd | SS; © megapixel.org | SS

73 East Rennell © Marci Paravia | SS; © Ethan Daniels | SS

74 Cedar Avenue of Nikko © Chiara Salvadori | SS; © Sean Pavone | SS

75 Longyearbyen © DonLand | SS; © Avatar_023 | SS

76 Eastern State Penitentiary © Alicia Dauksis | SS

77 Dinosaur Provincial Park © Elena Elisseeva | SS; © Pecold | SS

78 Glenwood Hot Springs © Glenwood Hot Springs

79 Lord Howe Island Group © photobyash | iStock

80 Bodega Colomé © Bodega Colome

81 Mongolia © rm | SS

82 Ashmolean Museum © Ashmolean Museum, University of Oxford

83 Ometepe © pniesen | iStock

84 Giant Buddha of Leshan © gringos4|SS

85 Molokai - Hawaii Tourism Authority

(HTA) © Tor Johnson; © Dana Edmunds

86 Prague Castle © Kajano | SS; © Boris Stroujko | SS

87 Xinjiang © Pikoso.kz | SS

88 Grand Bazaar © Alexander Tolstykh|SS; © Vitaly Titov & Maria Sidelnikova | SS

89 Ushuaia © sunsinger | SS; © jorisvo | SS; © meunierd | SS

90 Keukenhof © Mediagram | SS; © Keukenhof Lentepark

91 Bay of Fundy © Tourism New Brunswick Canada; © V. J. Matthew | SS

92 Haifa © StockStudio | SS; © Zhukov | SS

93 Victoria Falls © Przemyslaw Skibinski | SS

94 Via Appia © LianeM | SS

95 Yellowstone National Park © Tim Stirling | SS; © Krzysztof Wiktor | SS; © Lee Prince | SS

96 Lærdal Tunnel © LIUDMILA ERMOLENKO | SS; © Tatiana Popova|SS

97 The Pantanal T © Filipe Frazao | SS; BL © ckchiu | SS; BR © Joe McDonald | SS; © Filipe Frazao | SS

98 Grand Canal © Photobank | SS

99 The 'Falkirk Triangle' © Joop Snijder Photography | SS

100 KwaZulu Natal Coast © atese | iStock

Page 1 © manasaweeu | SS

Page 2 © Anatoly Tiplyashin | SS

Page 303 © Sean Pavone | SS

SS = Shutterstock.com

DT = Dreamstime.com

Photo credits have been listed according to destination number

First published in 2015 by New Holland Publishers Pty Ltd
London • Sydney • Auckland

The Chandlery Unit 009, 50 Westminster Bridge Road London SE1 7QY United Kingdom
1/66 Gibbes Street Chatswood NSW 2067 Australia
218 Lake Road Northcote Auckland New Zealand

www.newhollandpublishers.com

A record of this book is held at the National Library of Australia.

ISBN: 9781742576817

Managing Director: Fiona Schultz
Publisher: Alan Whiticker
Production Director: Olga Dementiev
Editor: Holly Willsher
Designer: Andrew Davies
Cover Photo: Jason deCaires Taylor
Printer: Toppan Leefung Printing Ltd (China)

10 9 8 7 6 5 4 3 2 1

Keep up with New Holland Publishers on Facebook
www.facebook.com/NewHollandPublishers